IRELAND'S
ARMADA LEGACY

Laurence Flanagan

ALAN SUTTON
GILL AND MACMILLAN
1988

First published 1988

Published in Ireland by
GILL AND MACMILLAN LTD
GOLDENBRIDGE · DUBLIN 8
with associated companies in
Auckland, Delhi, Gaborone, Hamburg, Harare, Hong Kong, Johannesburg, Kuala Lumpur, Lagos,
London, Manzini, Melbourne, Mexico City, Nairobi, New York, Singapore, Tokyo

British Library Cataloguing in Publication Data
IRELAND

Flanagan, Laurence
Ireland's Armada Legacy
1.   Ireland. Coastal waters. Shipwrecks.
Spanish Armada. Items associated with the
Spanish Armada. Catalogues, indexes
I.   Title
941.505

ISBN 0–7171–1593–3

Published in Great Britain by
ALAN SUTTON PUBLISHING
BRUNSWICK ROAD · GLOUCESTER

British Library Cataloguing in Publication Data
GREAT BRITAIN

Flanagan, Laurence
Ireland's Armada legacy
1.   England. War, 1588 with Spain.
Spanish Armada. Items in Ireland associated
with Spanish Armada.
I.   Title
942.05′5

ISBN 0–86299–473–X

Cover: A contemporary navigational map of Ireland, *c.* 1599, by Baptista Boazio, showing the treacherous
south-west coast where many of the Spanish ships, including the *Santa Maria de la Rosa*, went down.
Artefacts from the Ulster Museum.

Typesetting and origination by
Alan Sutton Publishing Limited.
Printed in Great Britain by
The Guernsey Press Company Limited,
Guernsey, Channel Islands.

Contents

Note

Chapters 4 to 13 of this book are divided into two parts: the first part describes the artefacts concerned in the chapter and puts them into their historical context; the second part catalogues the Ulster Museum holding in the chapter category.

All plates are referred to throughout the text by their catalogue number. References in the main text will also point the reader to additional detailed information contained in the catalogue entry.

In the Catalogue entries, the following abbreviations have been used:

d   diameter
l   length
h   height
w   width
mm   millimetre(s)
g   gramme(s)
kg   kilogramme(s)

CHAPTER 1
The Armada

Philip II acceded to the throne of Spain in 1556. In 1554 he had married Mary Tudor, Queen of England, a match which was intended to promote Anglo-Spanish friendship; in this it failed abysmally. Anglo-Spanish relations were too precarious to be improved by a mere marriage and Mary's persecution of English Protestants did little to endear her Catholic consort to her subjects. On Mary's death in 1558, her heir and half-sister Elizabeth came to the throne of England; the two protagonists in the drama of 1588 were in position, Philip in Spain, Elizabeth in England.

For years there had been an ongoing story of provocative minor incidents. English seamen, without overt royal support or approval, had yielded to the temptation of diverting as much of the wealth and treasure of the West Indies to their own pockets as possible, either by trade – despite the fact that the monopoly in this trade belonged to Spain – or by sheer piracy, seizing treasure-laden Spanish ships wherever they could on the high seas. If one of these excursions failed, the participants might pay the penalty by execution, sometimes being burned at the stake dressed in the yellow robes of heretics.

Occasionally there were more flagrant demonstrations of ill-will, including in 1579 one that could have had severe consequences had it been successful. On 17 July three ships from northern Spain landed a small, rather motley force of Spanish, English and Italian volunteers near Dingle, in the extreme south-west of Ireland. They were under the command of a so-called 'renegade' Irishman, James Fitzmaurice, or the son of Maurice Dubh, as he is called in the Irish account of the incident preserved in the *Annals of Loch Ce*:

> The son of Maurice Dubh, son of the Earl of Des-Mumha (= Desmond), came to Erinn in this year, and a few Spaniards along with him. They occupied Dun-in-oir in Mumha (= Munster); and when the Justiciary of Erinn heard this he assembled a large army, viz., the Earl of Cill-dara (= Kildare) and Captain Malbie, i.e. the Governor of the province of Connacht at that time and a great number of the Gaeidhel (= Irish) of Connacht, and the province of Laighen (=Leinster), with its armament, and a great number of Munstermen. When the sons of the Earl of Des-Mumha, viz., John, the son of James, and Shemus-na-tinol (= James of the musters), his other brother, heard that James, the son of Maurice Dubh, had come to Erinn, accompanied by the Spaniards, they raised an insurrection of war against the

Foreigners (= English) of Mumha; and the president of the two provinces of Mumha, and eight of the principal Foreigners along with him, were killed in their own territory. James, the son of Maurice Dubh, went on an expedition into the country of Clann-William. The Clann-William of the Suir, i.e. the posterity of the Red Earl, overtook him. They fought with each other. The son of Maurice Dubh fell there; and three of the Clann-William fell with him. The Justiciary went to Mumha, with this large army which we have mentioned, and it is not possible to reckon or calculate the towns, corn-fields and property destroyed in Mumha on that occasion.

The next summer, however, the awaited reinforcements arrived from Spain, but not in adequate numbers – clearly it was hoped that sufficient numbers of the Irish would rise in order to make a success of this attempt to throw off the English yoke. In the event, a mere 800 were disembarked from the Spanish squadron that sailed from Santander in northern Spain to Smerwick, commanded by the redoubtable Don Juan Martinez de Recalde. He, at least, was later to put this Irish experience to good use. He spent a week surveying the Irish coast after landing the force, then headed back to Spain; the force having sailed under the Papal banner, it had merely been 'lent' ships and money by Philip. The enterprise itself was a total disaster; the 'invasion force' set up their ordnance in a small fort overlooking Smerwick harbour where the English squadron, commanded by Sir William Wynter, soon found them. They proceeded to blast the expedition virtually into the water, using the relatively new tactic of maintaining a battery from the three larger vessels – the *Revenge*, the *Swiftsure* and the *Aid* – while three smaller vessels – the *Merlin*, the *Achates* and the *Tiger* – circled close to shore, firing their bow-guns, their broadsides, then their stern-guns, also keeping up an incessant barrage. Final capitulation came when an English army of 800 men arrived on the landward side and started up a fierce cannonade. A white sheet was waved from the fort; the small garrison surrendered. No promises were made and no quarter was given; the officers were held for ransom, the soldiery were slaughtered to the last man. The account of this in the *Annals of Loch Ce* is short and to the point: 'Spaniards came to Erinn, five or six hundred, to Dun-an-oir; and they all fell by the Justiciary.' The only man to gain anything from the débâcle was Recalde, who nine years later was grateful for his knowledge of Ireland. Some 390 years later, however, the National Museum of Ireland benefited when the excavators of the *Santa Maria* conducted a small excavation on the site of the fort and found some pathetic relics of the affair: some iron shot, a soldier's belt-buckle and the shattered remains of a small piece of ordnance which had, apparently, exploded.

Greater things were occupying Philip's mind than the slaughter at Smerwick of some volunteers who after all had nothing to do with him. In 1580 the King of Portugal died. Philip, a close cousin, seized his opportunity; the Duke of Alba was sent with an army to Lisbon while Don Alvaro de

Bazan, Marquis of Santa Cruz (and a Knight of Santiago) sailed up the Tagus in support. Interestingly enough the *Annals of Loch Ce* record this too:

> After the fall of the King of Portugal . . . King Philip, i.e. the King of Spain, sent his own guardian, with an army, to Lisbon; and the King of Portugal had no heir except a bastard brother, whose name was Don Antoine. And a battle was fought between Don Antoine and the Duke of Alva, the King of Spain's guardian, and the battle was gained against Don Antoine; and three or four thousand men were slain under Don Antoine, but he escaped himself from the battle; and Lisbon was taken against him. And King Philip came to Lisbon; and he has the city and the kingdom.

In one shrewd stroke Philip acquired not only undisputed control of the entire Iberian peninsula and the wealthy Portuguese colonies in the Pacific and the Atlantic, but also a very significant addition to his fleet – eleven intact, fully-fitted galleons, the nucleus of the squadron of Portuguese galleons that was to sail with the Armada eight years later, its flagship carrying the flag of the Commander-in-Chief. At this time, however, there was a more pressing use for these galleons; the one part of the Portuguese empire that had not yielded was the Azores, a cluster of strategically placed islands in mid-Atlantic, where a rival claimant to the throne of Portugal, Don Antonio, had set up his headquarters. From there, with the help of the French (he had already unsuccessfully sought the aid of Elizabeth), he hoped to launch an attack to wrest Portugal back from Philip. The French supplied a force of 6,000 soldiers, carried in 60 ships and under the command of Filippo Strozzi, a Florentine nobleman resident in France. This force set off for the Azores in 1582, some two weeks before the Spanish fleet, only thirty-six ships strong, sailed from Lisbon under the Marquis of Santa Cruz. Meanwhile Don Juan Martinez de Recalde was fitting out a support fleet at Cadiz.

When Santa Cruz arrived at Terceira, the second largest island in the Azores, the French force had already been there six days and heavily outnumbered the Spanish. Nonetheless all the Spanish commanders agreed to attack. To their intense frustration it was three days before there was any real action, three days spent chasing each other intermittently, as the wind allowed, and to little effect. Then, at last, occurred the world's first serious sea-battle between such large and heavily-armed ships, with the tactic of boarding the enemy uppermost in the minds of all the protagonists. The breakthrough came when Lope de Figueroa, in the *San Mateo*, broke line with the rest of the Spanish fleet. Strozzi could not resist the temptation; he bore down on the *San Mateo* with five of his strongest ships and pounded the Spaniard with shot for the two hours it took for the rest of the Spanish fleet to get into position. When they did, another three hours of unremitting bloody conflict took place. Eventually the French turned and fled, their commander, Strozzi, dead and his flagship sunk. Spain's newly enhanced sea-power had received a distinguished baptism in this action off Sao Miguel: Santa Cruz had lost one small dispatch boat and 224 of his men were dead; the French had lost eleven ships and between 1,200 and 1,500 had been killed.

The finishing touch, however, had to wait until the following year. In mid July of 1583, Santa Cruz arrived back at Terceira with a fleet of 98 ships and an army of over 15,000. Inside two weeks he had gained control over all the islands and headed back to Spain to be fêted as befits a conquering hero and to receive the title of 'Captain General of the Ocean Sea'. A small bowl, commemorating the victory, was recovered from the wreck of *La Trinidad Valencera*, one of the Irish Armada wrecks (Cat 9.51). This was an uncannily appropriate find, for it was in the aftermath of the Terceira victory that Santa Cruz himself conceived the notion of attacking England. He wrote to the King: 'Now that we have all Portugal, England is ours.' Philip's response was to invite Santa Cruz to draw up an invasion plan.

The proposals put forward by Santa Cruz in 1586 survive and he suggested a very impressive force: so impressive, in fact, that it would have been impossibly expensive to organise, equip and put into effect. He called for a force of 556 ships, with an additional 240 lighters and smaller boats to be carried by the larger. Of the 556, 150 were to be large sailing ships, 40 were to be oared galleys, of the type that had been so effective at Lepanto against the Turks in 1571, and 6 were to be galleasses, a new-fangled mixture of sailing ship and oared galley. To man these vessels he suggested some 30,000 sailors and, as the invasion force itself, a total of 64,000 soldiers. Costing a wholly impossible sum just short of four million ducats, this plan would have denuded Spain of every vessel needed to maintain the country's economy, as well as draining her of able-bodied men – regardless of whether the necessary skilled mariners could be found. Even the provisions required were a monstrous total – a shopping-list well beyond the most optimistic exponents of sixteenth-century food technology.

Although the details of Santa Cruz's scheme were impracticable, the basic concept appealed to Philip. He studied it, analysed it, criticised it and sought ways to cut down the enormous costs. The first and most obvious method seemed to be to save on the number of soldiers actually carried in the fleet and thereby to reduce the quota of ships and the cost of providing them. He already had an army in Flanders – a well-trained, battle-hardened army under the Duke of Parma. It would be much cheaper to transport this across the Channel under the protection of a strong fleet. This basic rethinking was followed by other changes; despite their contribution to the success at Lepanto, the showing of the galleys against Drake when he attacked Cadiz plus the advice of Philip's naval advisers indicated a great reduction in the numbers of galleys, from forty to a mere four, to be desirable. The relative sizes of the ships were increased, from an average of 500 tons to one of 700 tons and the number of guns to be carried was almost doubled. The rations to be provided remained, pro rata, more or less the same as in Santa Cruz's plan, but those to be carried by the fleet were, in actuality, for less than one third the number of mouths and were required to last for a campaign of only six months instead of eight. The shopping-list therefore appeared much smaller (though Parma's army, presumably, still had to be fed somehow). The weakness of the new model, however, was now somewhat different; added to the difficulty of sailing a large squadron successfully from Spain to England without falling foul of the English fleet, was the even greater problem of achieving a synchronised and successful rendezvous with an army in small barges and protecting its progress across the Channel from that same hostile fleet.

It was, therefore, this less grandiose plan that was to occupy Philip and the Spanish administration. Santa Cruz, despite the modifications to his original plan, was still to be the man responsible for bringing it to fruition. Or so he learned in 1587 when he was back in the Azores, escorting the Treasure Fleet; he was instructed to set sail with the fleet virtually as soon as he returned. He pointed out that it was impossible; he had not enough ships, not enough men, not enough guns, not enough money. His difficulties were aggravated by the fact that Drake had destroyed at least 24 ships in Cadiz, as well some 1,700 tons of barrel hoops and staves and the tuna-fishing industry of Portugal, during his enterprise of that year. Philip's difficulties were aggravated by the fact that while the reigning Pope, Sixtus V, was in theory totally in favour of the invasion, and was quite willing to reiterate his excommunication of Elizabeth, he was singularly unwilling actually to produce the million gold ducats he had promised. The unfortunate Marquis worked on, the subject of continual recriminations from Philip, while the fleet, its supplies and men were being assembled – a programme of commandeering foreign vessels to augment the Spanish ships available had been under way for some time. However, he failed to meet one imposed deadline after another. Eventually, in February 1588, he took to his bed, a broken man, and died on the 9th, 'universally mourned by captains and soldiers alike'.

Philip appointed the Duke of Medina Sidonia as his reluctant successor. The Duke was a very illustrious figure who had been awarded the Order of the Golden Fleece, the highest Spanish honour, normally restricted to reigning monarchs and princes of the royal blood. However, so reluctant was he that he used every possible tactic to evade the appointment; he pleaded that his health was bad, that he suffered from sea-sickness, that he himself (one of the richest men in Spain) was in debt, and as a last resort simply delayed answering correspondence. Finally, when he could no longer see any way of evading it, he set off for Lisbon, to carry out his orders. There, a month after his predecessor's death, he found everything in total chaos, although Santa Cruz had succeeded in augmenting his fleet until he had gathered 65 ships and 16,500 men.

Delay again began to succeed delay; money for equipment and wages remained in short supply; food continued to rot because of the delays. But the Duke did succeed in again augmenting the number of ships, guns and men until, on 25 April 1588, the Sacred Banner of the Crusade was taken with great formality and ceremony from the high altar of Lisbon Cathedral; on 9 May, orders were at last given for the Armada to sail. Even then, however, it was nineteen days before the wind was in the right quarter to enable the Armada to cross the bar at the entrance to Lisbon harbour.

Before departure the Duke had sent the King a full inventory of the fleet: 130 ships including 65 warships or converted large merchantmen, 25 transports, 4 galleys and 4 galleasses, as well as 32 smaller vessels, mainly fast dispatch ships. The fleet was arranged in 10 squadrons, according to source (e.g. Portugal) or type (e.g. the transports or urcas). Aboard the ships were 19,295 soldiers and their officers, and to crew the ships were some 8,050 mariners. The fleet was armed with 2,431 pieces of ordnance, of bronze and iron and of all sizes, as well as carrying enormous quantities of shot, powder, other weapons, food and all the other appurtenances of war. In many ways what the Duke had achieved in so short a time was little less than a miracle; this was the greatest task-force the world had yet seen.

Unfortunately, sailing splendidly across the bar at Lisbon was one thing (in fact it took two days for the entire fleet to cross it); sailing up to the English Channel was to prove very different. When the ships reached the open sea, they encountered a strengthening wind from the north-north-west, eventually reaching gale-force. The entire fleet was driven south until, after a couple of days, it was actually in sight of Cape St Vincent, at the extreme south-west corner of Spain. Eventually, however, the wind did shift to south-south-west and it was able to sail in the intended direction, towards its destination.

By the time it reached La Coruna, having failed to rendezvous with some expected victuallers, a large portion of the fleet, which had failed to follow the Duke in to harbour, had been caught by a storm and driven out of sight. The Duke's problems were compounded; he had to reconvene his fleet, organise the repair of those ships that had suffered severe damage in the storm (these included the *Santa Maria de la Rosa*, which required a new main-mast, and the *Girona*, which required new tillers and new rigging) and revictual all the vessels, in many of whose casks the water had turned green and foul and in many of whose sacks the biscuit was soaking. It is small wonder that from La Coruna he wrote a very despairing letter, in which he drew the King's attention to the almost universal inadequacies of the task-force, mainly in terms of human inexperience and incompetence. The King, however, was adamant; the enterprise was to go on, and with as little delay as possible.

Eventually, on the afternoon of Friday 29 July, The Lizard was sighted from the mast-head of the Duke's flagship, the *San Martin*. He caused to be hoisted on the main-mast a banner bearing the image of Christ Crucified, with the Virgin on one side of Him and Mary Magdalen on the other. The Armada at last entered the English Channel. Now to the worries about the weather, water and supplies were added worries about the English fleet and the projected rendezvous with the Duke of Parma.

The first sight of the English fleet was made on 30 July, dead ahead. At dawn there were eighty English ships astern; the Armada took up its famous crescent formation, with two galleasses on each wing, covering a full 7 miles of sea. This, of course, was also the first sight the English Admiral, Lord Howard of Effingham, had of the Armada: it was the largest enemy fleet he had ever seen. The apparent sizes of the two fleets, however, belie the fact that they were not finely balanced as can be suggested by three factors. Firstly, against the 130 ships of the Armada were ranged some 175 English ships; but among the 130 ships of the Armada were 23 urcas, or transports, and in addition to the 175 English ships were 22 victuallers, within easy reach of home ports. Secondly, the largest ship in either fleet was by no means the largest Spanish ship; *La Regazona*, the *capitana* of the Squadron of Levant, commanded by Martin de Bertendona, weighed in at 1249 tons, but the *Triumph*, under the command of Sir Martin Frobisher, was in fact the larger at 1100 tons, for the Spanish measure produced ratings at least 25 per cent higher than the English measure. Finally, the English fleet carried more guns in excess of four-pounders than the Spanish. Perhaps most importantly, the English fleet was close to home, did not have to carry, snail-like, its house on its back, and was fighting, literally, for Queen and Country.

The Armada sailed up the Channel, in its defensive formation, with the English fleet – who had the advantage of the weather – a few miles behind. Drake and Effingham divided their force into two columns, their intention being to shadow the Armada, pick off any stragglers, but avoid direct close-quarter confrontation. It was, of course, precisely this type of confrontation that the Spanish wanted most; they wanted to grapple the enemy after softening him up at close range with their heavy guns, then board. The English, however, were too crafty to allow this; they preferred to employ their longer-range guns to pepper the Spaniards from a safe distance and use their undoubtedly nimbler ships to dodge out of danger. The first blood went to the English; Recalde's *San Juan*, supported by *El Gran Grin*, commanded by Don Diego Pimentel, took on a squadron of English ships, including the *Revenge* of Drake, the *Triumph* of Frobisher and the *Victory* of Hawkins. The *San Juan* suffered damage, not fatal, but punishing enough, until the Duke in the *San Martin*, accompanied by the galleons of Portugal, sailed up to support him. The English made a tactical withdrawal.

The Armada sought to resume its crescent formation. In the process, however, the *Nuestra Senora del Rosario* (hereafter referred to as the *Rosario*) was rammed by another ship; her mizzen-mast came down, with it all her rigging and her mainyard, and she was totally crippled. But worse was to come. While the Duke himself was going to the assistance of the *Rosario*, a shattering explosion was heard. The *San Salvador* had blown up, whether by accident or sabotage is unclear, as so many versions of the incident exist. The results of the explosion, on the other hand, were crystal-clear: two hundred were dead or wounded; another fifty, it was said, drowned after jumping into the sea to avoid the inferno. While rescue attempts were being conducted, the *Rosario's* unsupported mainmast was carried off as well, leaving her totally helpless. Then, for whatever reason – and many blamed Diego Flores, the Duke's principal adviser – the Armada sailed on, leaving the *Rosario* and the *San Salvador* to their fates. The first two total losses of the Armada had been sustained, but not as a result of enemy action. Both were later towed into port by the English (with Drake rather sneakily getting the lion's share of the loot).

The next action was off Portland Bill. A group of English ships, including the *Triumph*, were spotted close to shore; the galleasses were sent in and the *Triumph* was briefly in danger; it was only by shooting at the oars that Frobisher managed to deprive the galleasses of their one advantage – that they did not totally depend on the wind – and escape. After another hot affray in which the Duke's *San Martin* was the main target, the Armada resumed its crescent formation and sailed on.

On 3 August both the English and the Spanish decided to change their tactics: the English to split their forces into four squadrons, the Spanish to land on the Isle of Wight and use it as a beach-head. The Duke explained his plans in a letter to the King and he also wrote to the Duke of Parma to persuade him to speed up his preparations.

The following day the galleasses were involved in another action that revealed their weaknesses. Going to the aid of a couple of stragglers, they were again subjected to a hail of shot, aimed mainly at their oars. In the event, Recalde's *San Juan* again led the support the galleasses needed and once more the *Triumph* was at risk. However, she escaped, apparently because the Duke failed to seize his opportunity, much to the disgust of De Leiva and many of his brother officers. As this encounter drew to a close, the Armada reformed, and continued to sail up the Channel, having been forced past its access to the Isle of Wight. On 6 August the Duke announced, despite opposing views voiced by many squadron commanders, that he intended to anchor at Calais and there join up with Parma's army. The contrary opinions were well founded, for the very next night, shortly after midnight, the English sent eight blazing fireships in among the Spanish fleet as it lay at anchor. Cables were instantly cut; panic set in, the fleet was in confusion. The following day's dawn showed it scattered, many of the ships without anchors. In the confusion the *San Lorenzo*, the *capitana* of the squadron of galleasses, had been involved in a collision which caused its rudder to foul on a cable and snap off. The commander, Hugo de Moncada, arranged to shelter in Calais, under the protection of the guns of the castle, and repair his rudder. Unfortunately he had no local pilot and did not know the approaches himself. The *San Lorenzo* grounded on a shoal and heeled over, helpless. There, after fierce resistance, in the course of which her gallant commander was killed, she was looted by the English. Finally the castle guns were turned on the English and the ship and her guns were left to the garrison and governor of Calais.

A group of eleven other Spanish ships meanwhile were receiving the undivided attention of more than a hundred English ships off Gravelines until the rest of the Armada sailed in to the rescue. Although the English fired broadside after broadside and inflicted grievous damage on the grotesquely outnumbered Spanish ships, by the time they withdrew they had not managed to sink or capture a single one. As night began to fall, however, the *Maria Juan* sank, while the *San Mateo* and *San Felipe* were dangerously low in the water and eventually drifted on to the sandbanks of Flanders. From the *San Mateo* the Dutch recovered a huge linen banner which was hung in triumph in the Cathedral at Leiden.

The *San Mateo* and the *San Felipe* were not the only ships which faced the danger of the sand banks; the entire fleet very nearly shared the same fate. The wind had strengthened and now blew from the north-west; the sandy coast came inexorably closer. Nothing but a miracle it seemed could save the Spanish. But just as total disaster seemed inevitable, the wind shifted to west-south-west. The Spanish weighed whatever anchors remained and moved into the clear waters of the North Sea. They still had not kept their rendezvous with Parma. What were they to do? Were they to regroup, sail back into the Channel and resume their invasion attempt? The answer came the next day: sailing instructions were issued to take the survivors home to Spain. The Enterprise of England had failed.

Sources Consulted for Chapter 1

Hennessy, W.M., *The Annals of Loch Ce*, London, 1871
Lewis, M., *The Spanish Armada*, London, 1960
McKee, A., *From Merciless Invaders*, London, 1987
Martin, C., *Full Fathom Five*, London, 1975
Mattingly, G., *The Defeat of the Spanish Armada*, London, 1983
Stenuit, R., *Treasures of the Armada*, London, 1974

CHAPTER 2
The Armada in Ireland

Spaniards came to Erinn, a very great fleet; and eight or nine of those ships were wrecked in Munster and Connacht; and Saxons killed all who were not drowned of the crews of those ships that were wrecked; and it is not possible to reckon or tell all that were drowned, and all that were slain in that fleet, on account of their number, and the quantity of the spoils got, of gold and silver, and of every kind of treasure besides.

Such is the terse account of the Armada in the Irish *Annals of Loch Ce*. It is true that after the Armada had emerged from the English Channel and set about the long and hazardous journey up the east coast of England and around the north of Scotland, many ships did come to grief on the coasts of Ireland. Including those that were wrecked off the Ulster coast, the total tally is in fact between twenty and twenty-four.

That the wrecking of so many Spanish ships, laden with stores and arms that could be valuable, and the landing of so many armed and trained Spaniards on an island somewhat scantily defended, exercised the English government of Ireland is revealed by a Commission from the Lord Deputy Fitzwilliam issued from Dublin Castle in September 1588:

Whereas the distressed fleet of the Spaniards, by tempest and contrary winds, through the providence of God, have been driven upon this coast, and many of them wrecked in several places in the province of Munster, where there is to be thought hath not only been much treasure cast away, now subject to the spoil of the country people, but also great store of ordnance, munitions, armours and other goods of several kinds, which ought to be preserved for and to the use of Her Majesty; and to the end there may be due inquiry had as well of the premises as also of the shipping which are or by any means may be recovered: we authorize you to make inquiry by all good means, both by oaths and otherwise; to take all hulls of ships, stores, treasures etc into your hands; and to apprehend and execute all Spaniards found there, of what quality soever. Torture may be used in prosecuting this inquiry.

It was not that the Spanish commanders had wilfully ignored the sailing instructions of the Duke that caused such devastation. Despite the fact that it is recorded that 1588 saw a particularly bounteous harvest in Ireland, 'the most plentiful in food and produce', the autumn of the year apparently was notorious for storms and strong winds; it was these that drove so many Spanish ships on to the west coast of Ireland, on which inhospitable cliffs and dangerous landfalls abound. While some of the Spanish commanders had some knowledge of the Irish coast – Don Juan Martinez de Recalde, for example, of the *San Juan de Portugal*, had commanded the flotilla of Italian ships which had landed a force of 800 men at Smerwick a mere nine years earlier – many did not; quite a number of the ships had already suffered from the dire weather and were in poor condition before their final catastrophe; the crews in many cases were weakened by hunger, thirst and disease. It was, therefore, almost inevitable that quite a large proportion of the Spanish fleet should perish along the Irish coast. It is perhaps more remarkable that so many did not and did in fact return safely to Spain, Recalde included.

From the day the Duke had issued his sailing instructions, the day-to-day story of the Armada's progress on its homeward way is a tale of a succession of disasters. The first blow to the demoralised Spaniards came the very next day, when the daily rations were cut to a meagre half pound of biscuit, half a pint of wine and a single pint of water. Only for the sick and wounded was there any supplement. To help eke out the water that was fouling in the barrels, the Duke ordered that the horses and mules on board – at one time an important part of the invasion equipment – should be thrown overboard, despite the fact that they might have made an important addition to the severely reduced rations. But the water situation was critical, so over they went.

To add to their misery, as they followed their instructions, the Spaniards sailed further and further north; as one of them recorded, 'In latitude 62 degrees it is not warm.' Latitude 62°, if his observation is correct, is north of the Shetlands, where the mean monthly temperature today is 54.3°F, compared to the 80°F or so that could be expected in Rome or Lisbon at that time of year.It seems in addition that 1588 was as bad for low temperatures as it was for storms and the Armada suffered not merely from fog but from freezing fog. This had the effect not only of lowering their morale still further and aggravating their physical debilitation, but also made it impossible to see one ship from another or to take sightings of the sun or the stars.

By 20 August the fleet, still together, had rounded the Orkneys. However, when the Duke sent a dispatch to the King on 3 September, he stated that in the previous two weeks they had had four nights of storms and seventeen ships had disappeared from view; 3,000 of the men were sick, not counting the large number of wounded, and many were dying. By the time he sent this dispatch, the first of those missing ships, the *Barca de Amburg* had sunk. She was a member of the Squadron of Urcas (rather unflatteringly translated as 'hulks'), mainly drawn from the Baltic, and serving with the Armada probably with the full knowledge and consent of their Hanseatic owners, and she was one of a group of four ships which had become detached from the main fleet. Two of her companions were also urcas, one *El Gran Grifon*, the flagship of the Squadron, the other the *Castillo Negro*, and along with them was a large Venetian merchantman, *La Trinidad Valencera*. Because of their use in long distance trade, between the ports of the north such as Hamburg and Rostock, the urcas were designed to carry as much cargo as economically as possible; they were sturdy, but by no means nimble. So, when pumping no longer availed to save the leaking *Barca de Amburg* when she foundered somewhere off the north coast of Ireland, at least there were ships nearby to take aboard her crew of 250. *La Trinidad Valencera* and *El Gran Grifon* took them aboard, an act which granted the ship-wrecked crew an all too short stay of execution. The *Castillo Negro*, meanwhile, disappeared into the dark and was never heard of again; unless she is the mysterious ship referred to in a notification by Geoffrey Fenton of 'such shippes of the Spanish fleet as perrished in September 1588' as 'one shippe wrecked near to Dunluce wherein about 300 men perished'. Her complement of sailors and soldiers was 313.

The final moments of the remaining members of the group were more accurately recorded. *La Trinidad Valencera*, having lost contact with *El Gran Grifon*, was caught in a bad storm on the night of 12 September. She sustained damage forward which caused her, in her turn, to take on such quantities of water that the pumps could not cope. She had no option, but to run for land, finding Kinnagoe Bay, at the eastern tip of Malin Head in north Donegal. Here she ran aground on a reef. *El Gran Grifon* fared little better. She ploughed on, taking a south-westerly course into the Atlantic, until on 7 September she was caught in a severe storm. This opened up seams already loosened by battle-damage and made it necessary for her simply to run before the wind. A diary maintained by one of the survivors (not certainly identified) records details of the horrendous trials which followed. First the wind carried the ship north for three days, then south-west for another three, until she was as far south as Galway; then the wind turned again and she was again carried north for three days. Meanwhile 'the wind was so strong and the sea so wild that the men were all exhausted and unable to keep down the water that leaked through our gaping seams'. A slight improvement in the weather enabled them to effect temporary repairs to the seams with ox-hides. Inevitably, it would seem, the weather then deteriorated again. After a few more days of tossing and turning the storm became so violent that their provisional repairs were unable to hold and the crew 'had to keep both pumps always going to keep the water down'. Eventually, after dodging among the Scottish islands and a final phase of incessant pumping and use of buckets, they came to rest on 27 September off Fair Isle, in the only safe anchorage available. Attempts the following day to beach the stricken ship failed, but, although the ship sank, the men were able with difficulty to get ashore.

Other ships of the Armada underwent similar vicissitudes. One of these was *La Rata Sancta Maria Encoronada*, a Genoese ship of 820 tons, of the Levantine Squadron and commanded by the redoubtable Don Alonso de Leiva, which had lost contact with the main fleet as early as the end of August. This, with its complement of 335 soldiers and 84 sailors, entered Blacksod Bay, Co. Mayo, on 17 September. In the storms of June, which had sent the Armada to seek shelter in La Coruna, de Leiva's ship had already suffered damage to her rigging (as well as losing four anchors); then, when the Armada finally entered the English Channel, it was *La Rata*, by dint of being mistaken for Medina Sidonia's *San Martin*, the *capitana general*, which received the gauntlet thrown down by Howard of Effingham and, consequently, was the first ship of the Armada to exchange shots with the enemy. Subsequently, she was engaged with the rest of the Levantine Squadron in the action off Portland Bill against Sir Martin Frobisher's *Triumph*. The effects of these actions, combined with the repaired rigging, left her in poor shape to contend with the vile weather of the Atlantic in September 1588. So, in need of respite and, even more pressingly, fresh water, she put into Blacksod Bay. Whether it was because of the lack of anchors, or her general unwieldiness, she dragged her anchor and was firmly and inextricably driven aground on a shelving beach. De Leiva successfully disembarked all his men and occupied a small castle at Doona, overlooking Blacksod Bay. He fired the ship so that no useful spoils would accrue to the enemy.

On 20 September, while de Leiva was thus occupied on Blacksod Bay, farther to the north, at Streedagh Strand, Co. Sligo, a great storm threw three Armada ships on the gently shelving sand and proceeded to pound them pitilessly and tear them to pieces. In all 1,100 dead were counted from the three wrecks, all belonging to the Levantine Squadron: the *Juliana*, of 860 tons, *La Lavia*, of 728 tons, and the *Santa Maria de Vision*, of 666 tons. The death toll must have been a hurried guesstimate, for there should only have been 764 soldiers and 212 sailors on the three ships – and of these, miraculously, some did survive, one of them possibly the best known participant in the Armada, Captain Francisco de Cuellar.

All along the west coast of Ireland similar tragedies were taking place. Seven ships took shelter in the mouth of the River Shannon and tried to obtain supplies of fresh water. They were refused permission to send landing-parties ashore and, despite the absence of English troops, they were too weak to force the issue and had no alternative but to put to sea again, despite the raging storm. At Galway the entire complement of the *Falco Blanco Mediano*, save only her captain, Don Luis de Cordoba, were taken prisoner and summarily executed; de Cordoba was spared because he might be ransomed.

Further south, in the 'shelter' of the Blasket Islands, another drama was being acted out. Lying off the westernmost promontory of Europe, this small group of islands, the largest of which, Great Blasket, is only 4 miles long, forms an imperfect protective screen for mariners seeking shelter. The islands also present a considerable scatter of hazards, aggravated by a formidable tidal race. It was here that Marcos de Aramburu, in the *San Juan Bautista*, vice-flagship of the Squadron of Castile, found himself at dawn on 15 September. The *San Juan Bautista* was a galleon of the Indian Guard, relatively fast, sleek and manoeuvrable, and well used to the Atlantic seaways. As she came in from the north, one vessel was spotted to windward, beating north, and another to leeward. The first was recognised as the *San Juan of Portugal*, flagship of Juan Martinez de Recalde and vice-flagship of the Portuguese Squadron, at 1,050 tons a substantial vessel. The other was one of the small, fast dispatch-boats.

Recalde was a seasoned sailor, not unexpectedly as he was a nobly-born Basque. He had not only commanded escort fleets of the Indian Guard on the long haul from the New World to the Old, served as second-in-command to the Marquis of Santa Cruz in the successful campaign in the Azores in 1582 and been Controller of the Royal Dockyards, but, most importantly, had also commanded the flotilla of ships which landed the force at Smerwick in 1580. During the fortnight he spent on this expedition, ill-fated though it proved for the landing-force, Recalde had thoroughly reconnoitred the adjacent coasts. Smerwick is only 6 miles from Blasket Sound and, fortunately for Recalde, the knowledge was to stand him in good stead.

In the teeth of a strong wind from the west it was impossible for any of the three ships to head for the open sea. Instead they were more likely to be driven on to the rocks and steep-cliffed islands that form the Blasket barrier. Suddenly Recalde gave up his attempts to beat to sea; instead he turned and drove his great ship straight at what appeared to be an impenetrably small and sea-surging gap between Great Blasket and Beginish. Aramburu could scarcely credit what he saw, but followed in blind faith. To his delight and astonishment, he found himself in a safe haven, where the two large ships and the smaller dispatch-boat could lie at anchor in peace; the only quarter on which they were exposed was the north-east, and a wind from that direction would be set fair for the open sea and Spain. A couple of abortive attempts were made to acquire water and provisions: the first resulted in the capture of the landing-party; on the second they nearly came face-to-face with 100 English soldiers. When they had been there nearly a week, the wind blew furiously from the west, causing the flagship to drift down on de Aramburu's ship and damage her lantern and the tackle and rigging of her mizzenmast. At mid-day on this day, 21 September, another ship, the *Santa Maria de la Rosa* entered the haven, but by another entrance on the north-west. She was clearly in distress, for as she came in she fired first one shot, then another. All her sails, except her foresail, were in tatters. After casting her sole surviving anchor, she rode peacefully enough until at two o'clock the tide waned; then the *Santa Maria de la Rosa* dragged on the anchor cables of one of the other ships and, without further warning, in front of the horrified crews of the two *San Juans*, she sank, with all on board, 'a most extraordinary and terrifying thing'.

With the *Santa Maria de la Rosa* another ship, that of Miguel de Aranivar (possibly the *San Bernardo*) had entered the 'haven' of Blasket Sound; shortly after the *Santa Maria de la Rosa*'s dramatic plunge, yet another, the *San Juan Bautista* of Fernando Horra, arrived with her mainmast gone. (One of the confusing factors in Armada studies is the number of ships bearing the same, or very similar, names. Here, in a relatively small anchorage in south-west Ireland, were gathered together three *San Juans*, two of which were *San Juan Bautistas*.) The following morning, when the situation could be properly assessed, it was decided to evacuate her crew and scuttle her. Recalde even proposed removing her guns. Interestingly one of the army captains on board was Don Diego de Bazan, a son of the Marquis of Santa Cruz. The eye-witness who recorded these events, de Aramburu, was given permission to take to sea and run for Spain. On this occasion discretion did prove the better part of valour, for Marcos de Aramburu did live to fight again another day. Recalde too returned to Spain, but he went ashore to die, having discharged his duties to King, country and his subordinates magnificently.

Eye-witness accounts of disasters can often be less than reliable, suffering every degree of inaccuracy from wildly extravagant exaggeration to discrepant minor details. In the case of de Aramburu's otherwise accurate description of the sinking of the *Santa Maria de la Rosa*, there is one relatively minor inaccuracy; she did not sink 'with all on board, not a person being saved'. There was, in fact, a sole survivor. In the words of an English contemporary record, there was 'no man saved but one, that brought us this news, who came naked upon a board'. This hapless soul was interrogated no fewer than three times, and we can guess what interrogation is likely to have entailed. He seems to have been a young Italian from Genoa, called Giovanni. The transcripts of his interrogations contain a number of discrepancies and improbabilities, but, as Colin Martin says, 'he was a lonely frightened boy trying desperately to please his captors, and so delay the dark fate which inevitably awaited him when they wanted to hear no more.' Much of poor Giovanni's testimony is laden with the names of grand Spaniards who sailed on the Armada and, in particular, on the *Santa Maria de la Rosa*; his interrogators, denied ransom and salvage, were intent, as a substitute, to gain as much propaganda as they could. For this reason they would have been happy to hear, and believe, that the Prince of Ascoli, an Italian princeling called Antonio Luis de Leiva, described by Giovanni as 'the King's base son', was among those who perished on the *Santa Maria de la Rosa*. The neat disposal of even an illegitimate son of Philip II and ten of his noble retinue would have considerable propaganda value. The fact that he appears to have survived the Armada, however, makes it unlikely that he perished in the inimical waters of Blasket Sound; he lived for a long time after the tragedy, for the most part in Flanders and Italy, having left his ship at Calais on a staff mission to the Duke of Parma. He had, indeed, written to his father from Dunkirk on 12 August, when the retreating Armada was already off the coast of Scotland.

Of the other survivors of Armada wrecks in Ireland one is of particular interest. Don Francisco de Cuellar, of whose previous career little is known for certain, joined the Armada at Lisbon, as a captain without a command. It was only with the general reorganisation at La Coruna that he did receive a command, that of the *San Pedro*. This ship was previously commanded by Don Pedro de Mendoza, who was himself transferred to the command of *El Gran Grin*, the vice-flagship of the Squadron of Biscay, which was yet another Armada ship to be wrecked on the Irish coast, this at Clew Bay, Co. Mayo. The *San Pedro* was a ship of 530 tons and a complement of 272 men of the Squadron of Castile. Her contribution to the various actions in the Channel is not recorded and she comes into prominence only because of the subsequent fate of her commander, though she herself did return in safety to Santander.

De Cuellar was one of the commanders arrested and actually sentenced to death for contravention of explicit orders to keep close formation after the débâcle at Gravelines. While the death-sentence was not carried out (he seems to have argued his case very persuasively, putting most of the blame on his pilot), he was removed from his command and transferred to the custody of the Judge Advocate, Don Martin de Aranda. While there is no positive evidence to prove it, most authorities agree that it was to the vice-flagship of the Levantine Squadron, a converted Venetian merchantman of 728 tons called *La Lavia*, that he was transferred. This, of course, was one of the three great ships so horrendously driven ashore on to Streedagh Strand, Co. Sligo. De Cuellar described his dilemma at Streedagh among other adventures in Ireland in a letter to the King, written when he had, eventually, a year later, arrived in Flanders:

> While I was looking on at this scene, I did not know what to do, nor what means to adopt, as I did not know how to swim, and the waves and the storm were very great; and on the other hand, the land and the shore were full of enemies, who went about jumping and dancing with delight at our misfortunes; and when any one of our people reached the beach, two hundred savages and other enemies fell upon him and stripped him of what he had on until he was left in his naked skin.

De Cuellar's account of his wandering sojourn in Ireland is not only an adventure story, but also an important document of social history. In accounts of Ireland in the late sixteenth century, the eye-witness is almost invariably English, with the inevitable result that the Irish resistance leader is dubbed an arch-traitor and most descriptions are, to say the least, unflattering. De Cuellar is quite frank about the roughness of the life he shared with the native population, but, on the other hand, he is equally frank about their kindness to him. The part of Ireland he found himself in was by no means securely under English rule; in fact it was the scene of constant guerrilla warfare between the Irish and the invaders. De Cuellar passed from the territory of O'Rourke to the territory of McClancy, both of whom were perpetually sparring with the English and both of whom were, perhaps for that very reason, well-disposed towards Spanish survivors. While with McClancy, probably at Rosclogher, Co. Leitrim, where he had a castle, de Cuellar shared the simple life of the native people, perhaps a little more debased than normal because the constant warfare involved enforced tactical withdrawals from the home comforts of the castle. (It must be remembered, however, that even the English in Ireland were quite poor, as is shown, for example, by the inventory of the household effects of Lord Deputy, Lord Leonard Grey in 1540, of which the editor remarks: 'so, although being Lord Deputy, and in all probability possessing more household effects than any other half-dozen persons in Ireland, yet his whole stock was inferior to that of an English country squire or merchant of the period'.)

While with McClancy, whose wife was very beautiful and showed him much kindness, de Cuellar noted:

> The custom of these natives is to live as the brute beasts among the mountains, which are very rugged in that part of Ireland . . . They live in huts made of straw . . . They do not eat more often than once a day, and this is at night; and that which they usually eat is butter with oaten bread. They drink butter-milk, for they have no other drink; they do not drink water, although it is the best in the world. On feast days they eat some flesh half-cooked, without bread or salt, which is their custom.

After leaving McClancy, having declined the offer of his sister's hand in marriage, de Cuellar and his companions travelled across country, eventually reaching the north coast and actually seeing the place where the *Girona* had gone down (and thereby confirming in writing the identities of some of those who had perished on her). After a disappointment when the O'Cahan, at Castleroe on the Bann, failed to provide a suitable boat, the company were eventually shipped to Scotland with the assistance of the Bishop of Derry, Redmond Gallagher. From there, but not without difficulty and further hair-raising incidents, he eventually reached Flanders and, on 4 October 1589, he wrote his famous letter to the King.

Sources Consulted for Chapter 2

Calendar of Carew Manuscripts
Calendar of State Papers (Ireland)
Flanagan, L., Martin, C. and Stenuit, R., *Tresors de l'Armada*, Brussels, 1985
Hennessy, W.H., *The Annals of Loch Ce*, London, 1871
McKee, A., *From Merciless Invaders*, London, 1987
Martin, C., *Full Fathom Five*, London, 1975
O'Reilly, J.P., 'Captain Cuellar's Narrative', *Proc. Roy. Irish Acad.*, 1893
Stenuit, R., *Treasures of the Armada*, London, 1974

CHAPTER 3
The
Excavations

In addition to contemporary accounts there is now the legacy of the wrecks themselves. Three wrecks have now been excavated and three others have been precisely located, with some guns recovered from one.

While the general locations of several of the Irish wrecks were known, the first to be accurately located by material observed was the *Girona*. She was a galleass, a special adaptation of the Mediterranean oar-propelled galley, fitted with sails as well, the notion being that if there was no wind she could be manoeuvred by oars. (In the course of the fighting in the Channel there was, indeed, an occasion when the wind died completely and the galleasses looked fair to come into their own; the English, however, also overcame the problem, using their long-boats to tow their fighting ships.) One galleass, the *San Lorenzo*, grounded at Calais was described by an eye-witness as being 60 paces long, with 'oares, sales and ship red'. She carried 120 sailors, 169 soldiers and 300 oarsmen. Her armament consisted of fifty guns and all in all a galleass was a formidable fighting vessel – in the right context. The Atlantic, however, did not seem to provide the right conditions, although of the four galleasses in the fleet two did manage to get back to Spain.

The wrecking of the *Girona* herself was the greatest single disaster in the whole Armada story, with the loss of nearly 1,300 Spaniards, including, among those previously rescued from other wrecked Armada ships, the retinue of Don Alonso de Leiva, among which were men from some of the noblest families in Spain. Descriptions of her location in documentary sources were vague, contradictory even. However, on the north coast of Co. Antrim, near Bushmills, there are clearly marked on the Ordnance Survey maps a Spaniard Rock, a Spaniard Cave and a Port na Spaniagh.

It was this collection of names which first attracted Robert Stenuit, a professional diver and historical researcher, to the site and it was in 1958 that he initially heard of the *Girona*. In June 1967, the *Girona* now bearing three

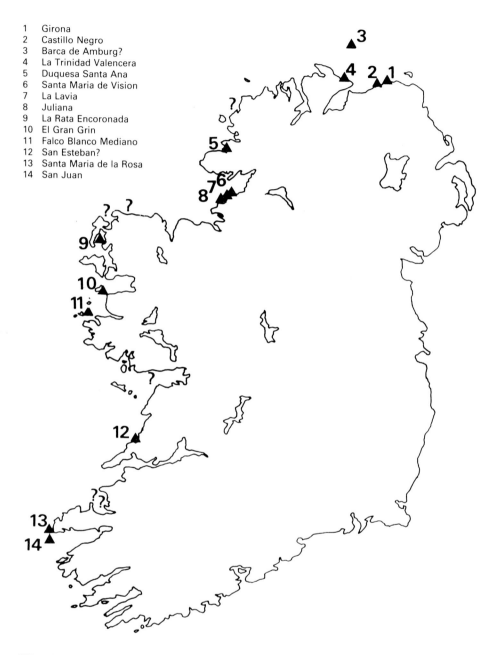

1   Girona
2   Castillo Negro
3   Barca de Amburg?
4   La Trinidad Valencera
5   Duquesa Santa Ana
6   Santa Maria de Vision
7   La Lavia
8   Juliana
9   La Rata Encoronada
10 El Gran Grin
11 Falco Blanco Mediano
12 San Esteban?
13 Santa Maria de la Rosa
14 San Juan

Wreck-sites of the Spanish Armada

stars in his wreck-file, he visited Port na Spaniagh and made his first dive. The first artefact he found, and recognised, was a lead ingot; next the barrel of a bronze gun, followed by another, complete with breech-blocks; and finally a copper coin. He knew he had found the wreck of the *Girona*. At the end of April the following year, Stenuit returned to the site; with him this time in addition to Marc Jasinski, an expert photographer both above and below water, were a full team and full equipment.

In summer the North Antrim coast can be beautiful and the Atlantic for short spells as smooth and unruffled as a millpond, but these ideal conditions do not often occur for long stretches. The submarine geography of Port na Spaniagh, moreover, is not one of smooth sand; it is a boulder-strewn chaos with forests of seaweed. A winter storm can move 40 ton boulders from one area to another with the greatest of ease and the geography is anything but static. It was here that the excavation of the *Girona* took place. The only blessing was that the water is shallow, as the ship had found to her cost when she struck the barely submerged tip of Lacada Point. In the event the work took two seasons, involving 6,000 hours of diving.

The results of the excavation were spectacular: two pieces of bronze ordnance and the muzzle of a third; an assortment of navigation equipment; 405 gold coins and 756 silver coins, as well as 115 of copper; a selection of small arms and many fragments of elaborately decorated silver-ware. The major discovery, however, was a fantastic hoard of Renaissance jewellery – gold rings, pendants and chains – which forms a considerable addition to the known collections of this type of jewellery. Of the ship herself, however, not one plank was preserved, partly because of the shallowness of the water and partly because of the exposed nature of the wreck-site; as the wreck broke up pieces would simply float or be carried away. One of the more important aspects of the *Girona* excavation, however, was that it became an invaluable precedent; for the first time salvage from a wreck was not sold off, at public auction, to the highest bidder. Instead it was sold to the Ulster Museum in Belfast at an agreed valuation and more recent finds from the site have also, encouragingly, met the same fate.

If Port na Spaniagh can be rough and diving at times difficult, how much more so is the case in Blasket Sound, where, after incredible trials (and errors), Sydney Wignall eventually located the wreck-site of the *Santa Maria de la Rosa*. The attractions of the *Santa Maria de la Rosa* were threefold: it was an almiranta, a vice-flagship, and likely to be carrying official, as well as personal, treasure (the *Girona*'s treasure was all the personal property of those on board); it was in at least 30m of water, which made it likely that some, at least, of the hull would be preserved; and it had sunk immediately, without being battered to pieces or falling apart.

Against these advantages had to be weighed the fact that as she was in deep water the actual diving time spent working would of necessity be much shorter; and the fact that, despite the presence of an expert eye-witness, de Aramburu, whose record is still extant, and of an actual survivor, the unfortunate Giovanni, her exact location in the 4 square miles of Blasket Sound was unknown.

The search began in 1963, with a preliminary reconnaissance led by Des Brannigan of Dublin, which failed to find the wreck. Resumed searching in the summer of that year again failed to find the wreck-site, but confirmed the hazards of diving in Blasket Sound, when Sydney Wignall, surfacing from a dive as the tide was on the turn, was almost carried out to sea. Another party failed when they searched briefly in 1964, but their presence suggested to Wignall that he should try to arrange some sort of protection, which on this occasion he did by arranging an exclusive-rights contract with the Spanish Government. Notwithstanding this contract, other divers, independent of Wignall, returned in 1967 and claimed to have found the site, but were unable to relocate it. This prompted an all-out attempt to find it in 1968, in which Wignall and his team were joined by John Grattan and a team of service divers, with the intention of conducting an extensive as well as intensive swim-line search.

Even this systematic and highly disciplined procedure seemed likely to fail until, after a full month, a large anchor, some 4m long, was found, with one fluke missing and the ring burst. Soon afterwards, they found the lower part of a second anchor, followed by a third, then a fourth, but still with no sign of a wreck. At this juncture John Grattan had to leave, then Wignall; despite near despair and the serious temptations presented by alternative sites, the remnant of the team resolved to continue. The breakthrough seemed to come with their reconsideration of a mound of stones that had been noted a month previously. Among it they found great piles of iron shot, lead musket shot, six of the (by now) classic Armada lead ingots and one of a very large rectangular form. The rest of that season was devoted to a survey of this, now recognized as a ballast-mound.

The next year, 1969, the team returned, this time with a 16m diving boat, the *Jimbell*. One problem which exercised them was that, although they had found iron shot, they had found no guns to fire it. Could it be, they wondered, that instead of finding the *Santa Maria de la Rosa*, as they had hoped, they had found instead Recalde's scuttled *San Juan*, the captain having succeeded in salvaging its ordnance? This question was soon resolved, when they found two pewter plates inscribed 'MATUTE'. It was known from documentary sources that Francisco Ruiz Matute had been a captain of infantry aboard the *Santa Maria de la Rosa*, in charge of a company of ninety-five men of the crack Sicilian tercio. They also found several arquebuses as well as a larger-bored musket and, somewhat gruesomely, under a 350mm pewter plate, the legs, pelvis and ribs of an unfortunate sailor who, they conjectured, must have been crushed to death by ballast when the ship so suddenly sank. Unfortunately little of the material from the *Santa Maria de la Rosa* has survived, which serves as a brutal reminder that, before commencing the excavation of any ancient wreck, it is vital to have adequate conservation facilities organised. The artefacts which survived are preserved in the Ulster Museum.

The greatest contribution made by the excavation of the *Santa Maria de la Rosa*, or rather of that part which was located, is the information it revealed about sixteenth-century ship construction. Under the 30m long ballast-mound it was hoped to find preserved part, at least, of the hull, an event which in fact occurred. The mound was large because ships of this period were innately top-heavy; the massive masts, with their great weight of sail, and the guns required a counterbalance to keep the ship upright; in consequence a ship of this nature had to carry a quarter of its weight as ballast. Carefully shifting the ballast, the excavators noted that it had been carefully packed, almost in the form of drystone walls, partly so that it would not shift, as the ship pitched and rolled, and partly so that it could readily be moved to facilitate inspection of the lower timbers. For this purpose it was arranged so that it could easily be removed from the top.

Interestingly, just forward of the mainmast, as might be expected in a sixteenth-century ship, were found traces which hinted at the location of the galley: charcoal from the galley fire, seemingly simply laid on the ballast without the formality of a special brick structure such as was found on the English *Mary Rose*; great piles of brushwood, presumably for kindling; and considerable quantities of food remains – bones of sheep, cattle and chickens, not to mention a brazil-nut which does survive.

While the *Santa Maria de la Rosa*'s precise resting-place took years of hard work to locate precisely, that of *La Trinidad Valencera* was literally stumbled upon, more or less by accident, though many had deliberately tried to find it. In February 1971 members of the City of Derry Sub-Aqua Club were holding a training dive in Kinnagoe Bay, in North Donegal. 'Keeping your eyes peeled for *La Trinidad Valencera*' was almost a club joke – until, that is, one of the divers discovered a piece of ordnance resting on top of a rock. This caused a flurry of activity and soon other guns were spotted. Since one of these bore the royal arms of Philip II of Spain, the inscription '*Philippus Rex*' and the date 1556, they were in no doubt that they had, in fact, found *La Trinidad Valencera*.

At 1,100 tons, *La Trinidad Valencera* was the fourth largest vessel in the entire fleet. Originally a Venetian merchant ship, she entered a Sicilian port in 1587 and was immediately commandeered to take part in the Armada. After her impounding, she was equipped with a supplement of 10 to her original 32 guns and, in addition to her crew of 79, she carried a force of 281 soldiers.

Fortunately there survives in the Archives in Simancas a detailed manifest of additional material she carried as an invasion transport, detailing her supplies and equipment, including three very handsome 50 pound siege-guns from the royal siege-train of Philip II and a Turkish gun, presumably one of the spoils of Lepanto. After she ran aground on the reef in Kinnagoe Bay, she sat for two days until, on 16 September, her back was broken and she fell apart.

From the outset, the City of Derry Sub-Aqua Club resolved that the excavation of *La Trinidad Valencera* was to be a properly conducted scientific undertaking. Colin Martin, of St Andrews University, was invited and agreed to act as archaeological director. The project turned into a model of cooperation between individuals and institutions; the BBC filmed it and thereby helped support it; the Ulster Museum provided conservation; Magee University College provided facilities and Allied Irish Banks provided some much needed money. The excavations produced considerable information about Armada ships, particularly with regard to subjects such as rigging and life on board. The fate of the ship's company provided evidence of the harshness of sixteenth-century life, for the greater part of the crew were tricked into laying down their arms on promise of safe conduct; they were then literally stripped of everything they wore and massacred.

While no substantial part of the hull had survived intact, some of the planking did. This showed that the fastening was by means of metal rivets rather than wooden dowels, unlike the *Santa Maria de la Rosa* and, indeed, the bulk of ships of the period. Overall the most notable feature of the site was the preservation of organic materials, including items of ship's furniture and fittings; the range of blocks, hearts and cordage is so far unparalleled in any Irish Armada wreck. Even more fascinating is the quantity of textiles, fragments of garments of wool, silk and velvet. The surviving items of invasion equipment include a tent and pegs and lanterns of two kinds, tallying remarkably with the written manifest. All in all the material from *La Trinidad Valencera* is complementary to that from the *Girona*, and even to the information from the *Santa Maria de la Rosa*. Like the material from the other two excavated wrecks, the material so far excavated from *La Trinidad Valencera* has been preserved in the Ulster Museum, by agreement with the Irish Government.

In 1985 the wrecks of the three ships on Streedagh Strand were located by the Streedagh Armada Group using sophisticated equipment. The identifications of the wrecks from newly analysed archival material showed that they were those of the *Juliana*, *La Lavia* and the *Santa Maria de la Vision*. So far only three gun-barrels have been raised because of legal complications, aggravated by the lack of assured conservation facilities; these are two bronze pedreros, specially constructed to fire the stone shot that abounds on Armada wreck-sites, and a handsome saker dated to 1570. The intact rudder of the

Juliana was revealed, but not lifted; it was 12m tall, with iron pintles still in position. There is no doubt that this could be a most rewarding site, but only if adequate conservation facilities are available.

Ireland's Armada legacy is therefore an extremely valuable one and constitutes a resource that must be exploited with care and responsibility. Its preservation is all-important, whether that preservation be on the seabed or, after due and adequate treatment, in museums that can provide adequate facilities for preservation, research and display.

Souces Consulted for Chapter 3

Flanagan, L., Martin, C. and Stenuit, R., *Tresors de l'Armada*, Brussels, 1985
Martin, C., *Full Fathom Five*, London, 1975
Martin, C., 'La Trinidad Valencera: An Armada invasion transport lost off Donegal', *International J. Nautical Archaeol.*, 8(1) 1979
Stenuit, R., *Treasures of the Armada*, London, 1974

CHAPTER 4
The Ships and their Equipment

The vocabulary of ships and shipping, sailors and the sea is an arcane one; few landsmen would recognise a futtock, a deadeye or a parrel. The delightful story told by Homer in the *Odyssey* leaps to mind as a gentle classical reminder of the classic division between those who go to the sea in ships and those who do not. In this incident Odysseus was instructed by the Seer Teiresias:

> You must take a well-cut oar and go on till you reach a people who know nothing of the Sea and never use salt with their food, so that our crimson-painted ships and the long oars that serve those ships as wings are quite beyond their ken. And this will be your cue – a very clear one, which you cannot miss. When you fall in with some other traveller who speaks of the 'winnowing-fan' you are carrying on your shoulder, the time will have come for you to plant your shapely oar in the ground.

In the sixteenth century, as in previous millenia, it took a great deal of courage to board a sailing-ship, even without the added hazard of holds full of gunpowder and enemies with hostile dispositions. A sailor would be totally dependent on the wind and his chances of knowing exactly where he was at any given time were severely limited by the navigation equipment at his disposal. These simple and basic facts explain a lot about the vicissitudes suffered by the Armada and about its ultimate failure. They also help to explain why, in the weather conditions prevailing in late summer 1588, so many Armada ships came to grief on the western shores of Ireland.

The century or so immediately preceding the Spanish invasion attempt had seen many innovations in the design and building of ships. One of the most significant factors, in this as in so many other things, had been the discovery of America and the continuing increase in transatlantic traffic and trade. The repercussions for ship design and construction, navigation, victualling and basic attitudes to sea-faring were enormous and the rewards for successful solutions to these problems were equally large.

There were many different strands to be woven together in the ship-evolution process. Navigation in the Mediterranean, for example, was to a very large extent coastal, in well-known waters. Naval warfare in the Mediterranean had evolved its own traditions which, like most, were innately conservative. Strangely it was a victory that reinforced these traditions: the great victory of Lepanto in 1571, which had broken the naval power of the Turks in the Mediterranean, had been a classic sea-battle of that region, between two opposed forces of oared galleys. Traditional weapons had prevailed – but against other traditional weapons. Since nothing succeeds like success, it was to be difficult for the Spanish to learn the lesson that the days of the oared galley were over. And with this had to be accepted the notion that a sea-battle was a land-battle surrounded by water, with as its main objective the boarding of enemy ships, culminating in hand-to-hand combat by soldiers.

A ship is basically a floating container for men, supplies and equipment: it has been described as 'a concave body framed of timber, plank and iron work, and contrived into several decks and rooms fitted for the use of men, munitions and victuals'. To this 'concave body' – the hull – must also be added: sails and the masts to support them; the standing rigging to support the masts; and the running rigging to manipulate the sails. Further refinements to increase efficiency or safety include the provision of rudders, pumps and anchors.

While detailed descriptions of Spanish ships of the late sixteenth century are unknown and pictures tend to be rather short on detail, there does exist a treatise, published in Mexico in 1587, written by Diego Garcia de Palacio and recently translated and edited by J. Bankston. While it is rather short on real practical detail, it does give guidance about the general size and shape of the ships in question. As an illustration he chooses a ship of 400 tons. Of the 130 ships in the Armada only 12 were rated at between 350 and 450 tons, and so could be deemed directly comparable to de Palacio's model. Of the other 73 rated at over 200 tons (excluding the galleys and the galleasses) 65 were larger, up to a massive 1249 tons, while 8 were smaller. Even for these the model may be taken as a useful indicator of the ships' requirements.

According to de Palacio's specification (he works in terms of cubits, which he equates with 2 feet) a ship of 400 tons should be about 22m long and 10m in beam (width); the lowest, or first deck (the orlop, in English terminology), is to be at a height of nearly 3m above the keel, the next, the gun deck, nearly

2m above that and the upper, or main deck, nearly 2m above that again. While the author lists some of the parts of the ship, 'the fundamental timbers', such as the 'stern-post, keel, stem, futtocks, top-timbers, cant-frames' and the like, he does not dwell on them or describe them in detail. Similarly he does not describe the superstructures, the towering 'castles' fore and aft that are such a feature of Spanish warships.

His prescription for the masts requires the main-mast to be over 30m long, the fore-mast some 22m (the same length as the keel), the bow-sprit nearly 18m and the mizzen the same length and thickness as the bowsprit. The main-top-mast is to be about 15m (the same as one-and-a-half times the beam), while the fore-top-mast will be some 13m. This is a very substantial amount of mast; even with the main-mast secured to a mast-step as part of the keelson, over 6m below the upper or main deck, the main-mast with her top-mast stands nearly 40m above the deck. With a main-yard prescribed at some 18m and the yard for the main-top-sail at nearly 10m, that for the fore-mast at 16m and for the mizzen some 24m in length, it is small wonder, as Colin Martin says, that 'because of their top-heavy design and the weighty hamper of masts . . . ships like the *Santa Maria de la Rosa* had to carry a quarter of their own weight or even more in counterbalancing ballast'.

We know from literary sources that by the middle of the sixteenth century, carvel construction, with the planks laid edge-to-edge, had in general replaced clinker-building, where the planks overlap. That this was, in fact, the case has been confirmed by several excavated wrecks, not merely those of the Armada. The earliest wreck to show this trend is the so-called 'Woolwich Wreck', thought to be that of the *Sovereign*, rebuilt in 1509; here there was clear evidence that the clinker planking had been removed and replaced by carvel planking. The *Mary Rose*, which sank in 1545, shows a similar feature. In this case, the oak planks were securely fastened to the frames with wooden trenails, many of which had been made more secure by wooden wedges driven in for a tighter fit; these have held securely over four centuries. The butt ends of the planks were once fastened to the frames by iron bolts; these, however, have corroded away, while the trenails still hold the planking securely. Similarly, with the *Santa Maria de la Rosa*, the 75mm thick outer planking, of the small portion of hull that could be examined, was fastened to frames with trenails. These were studded in groups of two or three, each one carefully spokeshaved to a round section, with a wooden tightening wedge at each end. Again, as in the *Mary Rose*, iron bolts had been used to secure the butt-ends. *La Trinidad Valencera*, on the other hand, shows signs of rather less careful construction from several pieces of oak planking from the hull which were recorded. One section, over 4m in length, is 350mm wide and over 75mm thick; it had been fastened throughout with iron fastenings, some 14mm thick, set in pairs 200mm apart, the heads of which had been countersunk to

13.1 Salamander Pendant, gold and rubies, from the *Girona*. Gold pendant in the form of a salamander, with four legs and two wings; the scales, mouth, teeth, eyes and nose are clearly modelled. Of the nine table-cut and bowl-set rubies only three survive

13.4 Cross of the Order of Santiago, gold, and red enamel, from the *Girona*. Oval frame containing a fretted cross in the form of a sword with the hilt in the form of an inverted heart, the arms terminating in fleurs-de-lys. This cross belonged to Don Alonso de Leiva, Commander Designate of the Armada make a smoother underwater skin. The very regularity of these bolts was probably the cause of the lines of split and breakage observed in the surviving planking and, as Colin Martin says, 'the impression is one of routine mass-production rather than the intuitive work of a skilled ship-wright'. Certainly, the use of the iron fastenings, rather than those of wood, did serve to speed up and make cheaper the task of ship-construction; probably, in the case of *La Trinidad Valencera*, because its Venetian owner envisaged a limited, but profitable, life-span for his ship.

The *Santa Maria de la Rosa* and *La Trinidad Valencera* have, between them, provided more information about ship construction than simply details of the planking. On the *La Trinidad Valencera* site, a couple of sections of framing were observed, each about 200mm wide, corresponding to the spacings of the fasteners on the planking and suggesting that the hull was solid framed. Ribs observed on the *Santa Maria de la Rosa* site confirmed this; every second rib or frame was 200mm wide by 300mm deep, with between them a smaller timber fitting into the gap with only a few centimetres or so to spare. The *Santa Maria de la Rosa* produced yet more information about the ship's 'fundamental timbers'. Under the enormous mound of ballast they found the ship's keelson, which runs along the inner hull directly above the keel, and with it forms the backbone of the ship. The keelson was made up of carefully jointed lengths, 300mm broad by 200mm thick, with slots cut into the underside to hold the ribs or frames in position. Still in position were four stumps of the stanchions which supported the first, or orlop, deck, each fitting into a mortice-hole in the keelson.

The painstaking work on the *Santa Maria de la Rosa* yielded yet more information. Less than 12m from the bow of the wreck the excavators came upon a curious box-like structure. Underneath, it was found that the keelson, where it passed through the box, was double its normal thickness, but badly torn and splintered. They realised that they had found the main mast-step, but of the mast itself there was no trace. It was then recalled that, in the storm outside La Coruna, the *Santa Maria de la Rosa* had lost her main-mast and had to have a new one fitted. The box, therefore, had been constructed to keep the area free of ballast while this work was going on. The collapse of this replacement main-mast had almost certainly played a major part in the break-up of the ship. One other curious feature was also observed: two planks, slightly more than 6m long and each 300mm broad by 50mm thick, set on edge, one on top of the other, not fastened to anything. These were interpreted as being intended to separate the ballast, so that where it was arranged carefully, almost like a series of drystone walls, it could be systematically moved to facilitate inspection of the hull timbers and, if necessary, allow repairs to them.

We have long known, from the abundant pictures and engravings that have come down to us, that the ships in the Armada were, for the most part, three-masted; square rigged on the main and fore-masts and lateen rigged on the mizzen (that is with a triangular sail on the mast nearest the stern). This mixture of sail types was an innovation which achieved greater manoeuvrability and economised on crew numbers. It had been introduced at least by the time of Colombo; the *Nina* was lateen-rigged at the start of his voyage, but he had her converted in the Canaries, giving her square sails on the main and fore-masts, which improved her sailing qualities.

Needless to say, on none of the wrecks do masts or yard-arms survive; these, if they had broken free of the wreck, would simply have floated away to serve as another contribution to the flotsam and jetsam of sixteenth-century Ireland. De Palacio does, however, describe at some length the standing rigging of the ships, which gives a quite breath-taking indication of its complexity. He does, however, literally leave loose ends. The function of the standing rigging was to support the enormous lengths (and weights) of the masts, in all weather conditions. So, inevitably, for the main-mast a formidable amount of support was required. Attached to the uppermost wale of the ship (a stout timber fitted to the hull wherever greater strength was required), at more or less the level of the upper, or main, deck, are the chain-wales. To these, on each side of the ship, are attached 12 chains of four or five links and to each of these, by means of a dead-eye (usually a circular wooden block, scored to take a rope round its outside, and usually with three holes through which pass smaller ropes or lanyards), is fastened a 'shroud' – a rope of 60 threads 'rigged and made fast on each side, and spliced and lashed below the top', 'they stiffen and strengthen the mast, so it does not move from side to side.' In addition to these shrouds, three pendants were attached on each side, where the shrouds were secured to the mast. Each of these, according to de Palacio, was to be half the length of the mast and to end in a single block, through which was passed a runner, long enough to reach the deck, with one end terminating in a double block. Through this was rove another rope of similar length, also ending in a double block, to which was bound a one-fathom strop or sling. The strop and runners are finally to be made fast to a pin-rail, fixed to the side of the ship above the chain-wale. This, involving the use of 24 lengths of chain, 24 (or more probably 48) dead-eyes, 6 single blocks, 12 double blocks, nearly 700m of 60-thread rope, 70m of 40-thread rope and 70m of 24-thread rope is simply to steady one mast, albeit the main one, across the width of the ship. To secure it fore and aft, a stay of 180 threads is used, reaching from the top to the stem; here it is attached to a chain with a bull's eye secured to the hull, which will require over 25m of this very stout rope. When the needs for the other two masts and the topmasts are added to this requirement, the quantities of rope and tackle necessary seem enormous.

Next we have to take into account the rigging required to get the sails in position on the masts and actually make the ship move. For handling the main yard, a main halyard was required, of 60-thread rope (not totally surprisingly, since it had to raise a yard some 23m long, which was as thick at the middle as the main-mast itself, together with the weight of a main sail which, dry, would have weighed something over 3 tonnes.) The halyard passed through a large block with two sheaves at the mast head, then through one of the sheaves of a block attached to the 'knight' (a stout timber strongly secured at deck level, aft of the main-mast). Next it passed back up to the other sheave of the mast-top block, back to the other block on the knight and then to the capstan. The mechanical advantage achieved by the two double blocks, and of the capstan, would quite clearly be necessary for the task in hand. In addition, truss-ropes are required for 'hauling taut and having the main yard secure'; these are made fast to the parrel (a sort of primitive ball-bearing to make it easier for the yard to be hauled up the mast) and again are rove through double blocks. The requisite amounts of cordage and tackle had become quite incredible.

Needless to say, even the *Mary Rose*, when she was raised, did not emerge in pristine condition: her sails were not set, her masts were not standing. Because of her relative completeness, however, she has produced a vast amount of rigging elements. Many of them are strikingly similar to those from the excavated Armada wrecks and in some cases they fill in details not so far observed on any of those Armada sites. Much of it has apparently been preserved by its having been stored in a compartment on the orlop deck. Probably the most spectacular item is a spare set of parrels, suitable for a mast half a metre in diameter, and a section of chain-wale, still in position on the hull, with blocks and dead-eyes still attached to the chains. None of the Armada wrecks has so far yielded parrels, nor was any portion of a hull intact at a height sufficiently far above the keel for the preservation of chain-wales *in situ*. Despite this, blocks of concretion recovered from *La Trinidad Valencera* have contained lengths of chain, revealed by X-radiography (Cat 4.27), and this ship in particular has produced a range of blocks of various sizes; these range from one 650mm tall, sadly attacked by Toredo worm (Cat 4.3), to quite small blocks of some 225mm (Cat 4.4), with rope still rove. Despite the size of the very large block, the pins of these are of wood. It is only the double blocks from *La Trinidad Valencera*, one with the corroded remains of an iron hook or strop still in position, that seem to have been fitted with iron pins (Cat 4.6). There do survive from the same ship, however, two bronze or brass coaks. These are square-based, slightly pyramidal objects, with a circular perforation through the centre (one 60mm square, with a hole 22mm in diameter (Cat 4.10), the other 64mm square with the hole 35mm in diameter (Cat 4.9)) which served as bearings for blocks, so that the wooden sheave was not split or damaged by the iron or steel pin. Coaks it is believed were intended for larger blocks, performing heavier, more arduous tasks. From the *Girona*, where the preservation of organic materials was almost out of the question, a whole series of such objects has been preserved. They range from one a mighty 110mm square with a hole 42.5mm in diameter, through a succession of smaller sizes, represented by some fifty examples, to small ones a mere 37mm square with holes of just 17 or 18mm across (Cat 4.11–4.17). Such coaks, not apparently encountered on the *Mary Rose*, had been in use on Spanish ships since at least 1554, two having been recovered from the Padre Island wrecks.

Bronze sheaves, of which two were lifted from the *Mary Rose*, have not so far been discovered on any Irish Armada site, although one is known from *El Gran Grifon* on Fair Isle; *La Trinidad Valencera* itself yielded a large wooden sheave, which was made in four pieces and cunningly morticed and pinned together; 545mm in diameter, it had an enormous hole 101mm across, but again without the benefit of a coak (Cat 4.8) (This may have been associated with lifting tackle rather than rigging, as indeed some of the blocks may have been used for raising the heavy weights on board or the securing of guns at their ports.) One puzzling question is: if the very large block from *La Trinidad Valencera* was expected to perform without a bronze coak, what size of block would require the services of the largest coak from the *Girona*?

Dead-eyes are a further type of ship-fitting which appear on the *Mary Rose*, these normally accepted as being circular or pear-shaped pieces of wood which are scored on the perimeter to take a rope or chain loop and usually have three holes in the centre to take lighter ropes or lanyards. They do not appear, however, on *La Trinidad Valencera*, where they might be expected; instead, perhaps, there are a number of 'hearts'. These pear- or heart-shaped wooden blocks are similarly scored on the perimeter, but with only a single hole, sometimes circular, sometimes quadrangular, in the middle (Cat 4.21) and are more often associated with stays than shrouds; it is possible that the Spanish utilised them throughout. On the other hand, there was found on *La Trinidad Valencera* a rather more elaborate device, a euphroe, which was usually employed to create a 'crow's foot' – a pear-shaped block of wood with a series of holes in line up the face (Cat 4.22). The *Girona* produced two iron shackles, which are probably similarly related to the rigging (Cat 4.23–4.24) and also a group of objects which are likely to be the remains of eye-bolts, each consisting of a threaded bolt fitting into an iron, apparently threaded, sleeve (Cat 4.25–4.26).

Of the rigging itself, only a very minute proportion of the enormous quantity of rope required has been recovered; a little of it is still rove in blocks, one section free-standing, of hemp consisting of three strands twisted to the right, laid together to the left, and 30mm in diameter (Cat 4.28). As for the sails, not a single scrap has survived of the thousands of square metres of canvas which would have been necessary. This seems particularly strange on the *La Trinidad Valencera* site, where other, less durable textiles, such as silks and velvets, have survived.

Many other items of ship's equipment are known, of course. We know that sixteenth-century mariners used a capstan, a simple winch, with an upright wooden spindle and leverage bars, securely fixed to the decking, which could be turned by teams of men to assist with raising sails; not only does de Palacio refer to one, but Alonso de Leiva was actually injured by the capstan of the *Duquesa Santa Ana* in the course of his second shipwreck. Unfortunately, as yet, no item recovered from the Irish wrecks may be interpreted as such an object.

We know of anchors, not only from references to their loss, in, for example, the haste of attempts to avoid the fireships, but also from the fact that the sea-bed in Blasket Sound is littered with six at least. In addition two are known from *La Trinidad Valencera* (Cat 4.2) and one small one from the *Girona* (Cat 4.1). From the anchors observed – but in most cases not recovered, conservation difficulties tending to discourage the recovery of too many anchors – confirmation is readily forthcoming of their poor quality. The first anchor, some 4m in length, observed in Blasket Sound, had obviously proved unequal to its task; the ring had burst and one fluke was missing. This damage suggested it might have been one of the *San Juan de Portugal*'s, dating from the stormy morning of 21 September when the flagship broke free of her moorings. The second anchor encountered in Blasket Sound was also broken, only the bottom part of the shank and the two flukes remaining. The interpretation here was that it had belonged to the *San Juan de Castilla*, thus neatly conforming to the statement by Marcos de Aramburu in his log: 'We hauled in the other anchor, finding only the stock with half its shank.' Of the two anchors on the *La Trinidad Valencera* site, the slightly larger, at 5m long, had again lost a fluke. We know, incidentally, from her manifest, that *La Trinidad Valencera* had embarked an extra anchor, of '18 quintals and 105 pounds, weight of San Sebastian, at 150 pounds to the quintal'. In association with the smaller anchor was discovered a short length of anchor cable, while a section 7m long was found separately. This cable is substantial, a full 250mm in diameter, and composed of four strands laid left-handed round a heart rope; each of the main strands and the heart rope is composed of three strands laid right-handed (Cat 4.29). The anchor recovered from the *Girona* is relatively small and, while the flukes remain, the top part of the shank has gone – more probably as a result of 400 years at Lacada Point than a failure in service. De Palacio recommends that each ship should carry four common anchors, a mooring anchor (to weigh from 16 to 18 quintals) and a kedge anchor (light enough to be recovered by the ship's long-boat). The four common anchors were to be carried on the sides of the ship at the bow, the others inside it.

From the firsthand accounts of many of the survivors we know of the ship's pumps – usually in terms of their inadequacy, which, for example, forced *La Trinidad Valencera* and *El Gran Grifon* to seek refuge inshore. None of the recovered Armada wrecks has so far revealed information on their nature, but a Spanish Basque whaling vessel, sunk in Red Bay, Labrador, in 1565, has preserved comparative evidence. Here, in association with a pump well (designed to keep cargo, ballast and other objects sufficiently far from the equipment), were found the remains of the pump with a foot valve and leather flapper and a plunger consisting of twenty-one individual leather discs. De Palacio, interestingly, states clearly his preference for Spanish, rather than English, Flemish or Italian pumps. He also gives a timely warning of the dangers of 'corrupt air' in the pump well, and the advisability of testing with a lighted candle before entering and curing with a mixture of water, urine and vinegar.

Of ships' rudders we have direct evidence, in addition to the depressing records of rudder trouble, especially with regard to the galleasses; the Duke of Medina Sidonia himself reported:

> I will set sail as soon as the flag galleass (the capitana, the *San Lorenzo*) has been put in order, her rudder being broken. These craft are really very fragile for such heavy seas as these.

The wreck of *El Gran Grifon* yielded a single wrought iron rudder pintle; the entire rudder of the *Juliana*, at Streedagh, Co. Sligo, has been observed. All of 12m in length, this is a good indication of the scale of these vessels; since the *Juliana* was rated at 860 tons she was more than twice the size of the 'model' of de Palacio. On the rudder survived the nine iron pintles by which it was attached to the stern of the ship, the vertical pins engaging in circular gudgeons on the stern. Again, because of conservation problems, this has not yet been raised.

So far we have discussed essential parts of ships, but there were, of course, other pieces of equipment used on board, many of them required for repairs. De Palacio gives a formidable list of these items, ranging from 12 quintals of pitch, 250 pounds of oakum and 4 barrels of tar to a whole series of nails and bolts, as well as a fairly comprehensive list of tools. The manifest of *La Trinidad Valencera* itemises other emergency equipment actually loaded onto the ship, including 1,500 iron scupper nails and 32 pounds of assorted nails, including 510 for the side of the ship and 1,100 others. Among the items inventoried is a tool-chest containing chisels, adzes, planes, gimlets, hammers and saws of various kinds. Among the tools and equipment actually recovered from the wrecks are some items that positively correlate with these lists, some that may and others that do not appear to do so. Most of these, inevitably, were recovered from *La Trinidad Valencera*. Two items that do match up with the contents of the tool-chest are two iron hammers, one a claw-hammer, the other a spall-hammer (Cat 4.38–4.39). While they retain portions of their wooden shafts, their condition suggests it is unlikely that the other tools listed – the saws, gimlets and chisels – would survive given the lighter nature of the iron elements. Two wooden mallets (Cat 4.40) have survived as well, items listed by de Palacio as necessary for the ship's caulker. Two items that may relate to the repair of sails were a heddle (Cat 4.43) – a simple device for weaving, perhaps for the manufacture of small patches for the sails – and a weaver's comb (Cat 4.44). Quite apart from the risk of battle-damage to the sails, there was also the rather grotesque-sounding, but nonetheless real, possibility that rats might eat the sails or the spare canvas; it was one of the boatswain's duties to ensure this did not happen. An item recovered that may appear on *La Trinidad Valencera*'s manifest is a block of resin, presumably used as an ingredient in a waterproofing varnish (Cat 8.17). Several lanterns, of different types, are also listed in the manifest and parts of two distinct kinds were found (Cat 4.30–4.31). A number of iron nails and bolts of various kinds have also been recovered from the *Girona*, though it is difficult to say with certainty whether they had been used or were carried as spares (Cat 4.50). One item that certainly falls into the category of material for repairs is a roll of lead sheet, 0.5mm thick, weighing some 5.4 kg which was most likely intended for the patching of holes in the planking (Cat 4.37); a pair of rather handsome bellows (Cat 4.42), 445mm long, of which the wood, but not the leather of the body survives, may have been for the use of a blacksmith on board, or simply for encouraging the galley fire.

From the *Girona* comes a piece that combines the utilitarian with the symbolic and shows that design in some things changes little, if at all, over centuries and through cultures. This is a little silver boatswain's pipe, at one time a badge of office and a sensible means of communication, competing effectively with the noise of weather or battle. It is remarkable how similar this sixteenth-century example is to today's (Cat 4.33).

All pictorial representations of the Armada show the ships gaily flaunting flags and pennants of every shape and description. When *San Mateo*, a 750 ton galleon of the Squadron of Portugal, ran aground on the Flemish banks and was captured by the Dutch, a great linen banner was taken from her as a souvenir and is still preserved. In the manifest of *La Trinidad Valencera* there is a reference to a linen or cotton banner for the mast-head. However, from the wreck-site was recovered what appears to be a portion of a banner or flag which most surprisingly is in wool. The portion which has been reconstructed is over a metre long and, apparently, depicts an eagle, in appliqué wool of a yellowish colour (Cat 4.32).

Of the 130 ships that composed the Spanish Armada 85 were sailing ships of more than 200 tons: some were designed and built as warships; some were merchantmen refitted as warships; others, like the 23 in the Squadron of Urcas were simply freighters or transports, used as such to carry supplies for the task-force. In general terms, where a difference in design existed between warships and merchantmen, it was that the latter tended to be 'rounder', or broader in the beam, than warships, being intended to carry as much cargo as profitably as possible. They, therefore, tended to be less readily manoeuvrable and generally clumsier. Although the two largest ships in the fleet, the *Regazona*, originally a Venetian merchantship of 1,249 tons, and Miguel de Oquendo's *Duquesa Santa Ana*, 1,200 tons and *capitana* of the Squadron of Guipuzcoa, did in fact return safely to Spain, the greatest incidence of destruction was among the larger ships: of 43 ships over 600 tons, 23 perished, while of 42 between 600 and 200 tons only 8 were lost. Of the large ships that sank or were otherwise lost (like the *San Salvador* which, after a disabling explosion, was captured by the English), several, such as the *Santa Maria de la Rosa*, built in San Sebastian in 1586/7, were relatively new ships; obviously the major factor in their demise was not age or decrepitude. Nor was the place of origin the sole factor; ships from Venice or Ràgusa or Rostock were as likely to perish as ships from Spain or Portugal. Two groups do, however, stand out as being particularly successful. The ten galleons of the Indian Guard, serving in the Squadron of Castile, and ranging in size from the almirante, *San Juan Bautista*, at 750 tons to the *Duquesa Santa Ana*, at 250, fared well. Only one of these galleons, one of the ubiquitous *San Juans*, this of 530 tons, failed to return, though she was not, as has often been supposed, one of the three ships wrecked on Streedagh Strand, Co. Sligo. The Portuguese galleons, as might be expected of ships built primarily for service in the Atlantic, were similarly durable, with only one lost on the homeward journey, the *San Marcos*, of 790 tons, possibly off Ireland. Two others, the *San Felipe* and the *San Mateo*, of 790 and 750 tons respectively, shared a fate that at one stage seemed likely for the entire fleet: they grounded on the Flemish banks and were captured by the Dutch.

A surprising number of the Urcas perished, despite being designed for and well-used to the turbulent seas of the north. Of the 23 listed in the Inventory, ranging in size from the *Castillo Negro*, at 750 tons, lost off Ireland, to the tiny *Ventura* at 160, which actually did get back to Spain safely, 6 were lost. These included the *San Pedro Mayor*, a hospital ship of 581 tons, which had successfully sailed round the north of Scotland and Ireland only to run aground in Devon. The Urcas were essentially non-combatant and were normally afforded a position of safety in the middle of the fleet.

In addition to all these sailing ships, there were two special squadrons in the Armada. One consisted of the Galleys of Portugal, the inclusion of which may have been a sentimental gesture to the old traditions of Mediterranean sea warfare; it was certainly not a very practical contribution to the strength of the fleet, for not one of them made it as far as the Channel. One, the *Diana*, was actually wrecked at Bayonne. The other squadron consisted of four mighty galleasses, actually very powerful fighting ships. Each was equipped with 50 guns and, in addition to the normal pattern of square and lateen sails, banks of oars, manned by 300 men in shifts, to propel the ship when becalmed. These even allowed it to take the offensive against other becalmed ships, an advantage negated when the English used long-boats to tow their wind-deprived galleons. One of the galleasses, the capitana, *San Lorenzo*, ran aground at Calais and was actually visited by an English seaman, Richard Tomson. A lieutenant on the *Margaret and John*, he was a regular merchant seaman, whose experience evidently included some in the Mediterranean. He provides us with an eye-witness description of the stricken ship. He describes her keel as being 60 paces long – presumably about 50m – with 25 oars on each side; he also makes the observation that the 'oares, sales and ship' were red and attributes to her '64 peices of artillerie'. By and large the galleasses were not as effective as had been hoped, partly because of the frailty commented on by Medina Sidonia; of the four included in the fleet, two did manage to return to Spain, but one of these, the *Zuniga*, arrived in great distress at Le Havre where she lay unserviceable for nearly a year. One of those wrecked was, of course, the *Girona*, since located at Lacada Point, Co. Antrim, although none of her structure was preserved.

While many of the ships in the mighty Armada were plainly unsuitable, and many others proved to be, the assembly of such a force was an incredible *tour de force* of management and logistics, as well as a considerable drain on the Spanish exchequer. In many ways the assembling of this mighty force was as much a piece of conspicuous consumption on the part of Philip II as the wearing of a heavy gold chain was on the part of many of his loyal noblemen. The Americas provided Spain with a great deal of wealth, although some of it had been diverted into the English coffers, and in the years leading up to the Armada Spain had been undergoing a more or less continuous ship-replacement programme, largely because of the continuing threat of the Turks and the need to keep them contained in the Eastern part of the Mediterranean. To make things worse, many of the raw materials of war were becoming hard to come by in the Mediterranean lands. Much of the timber for ship-building had to be imported; in the sixteenth century timber from northern Europe was arriving in Seville in boatloads of planks and beams and for the building of the Armada Philip had even sought wood from Poland. An indication of the resources required for shipbuilding is contained in an account of a visit to Lisbon in 1604, where a carrack of 1,500 tons under construction is discussed:

> The Portuguese used to make many more of them. The amount of wood which goes to make one is quite incredible: a forest of many leagues would not suffice for two. Three hundred

men working on a single ship can hardly finish it in a year. The iron to provide nails and other necessary metalwork weighs 500 tons. For the mast they choose eight of the greatest and tallest pine trunks and bind them together with hoops of iron.

While 1,500 tons is very large, it is only 250 tons greater than the largest ship in the Armada, the *Regazona*.

The volume of ship losses, even in normal trading, cannot be overlooked. In the course of a mere eighteen years at the turn of the sixteenth century, the number of 'insurance claims' relating to Venetian shipping amounts to 1,000 cases, of which about two-thirds relate to wrecks or captures by pirates. As far as Spain was concerned, after the Djerba débâcle in 1560 when twenty-eight galleys were lost, followed in 1562 by the loss of the entire fleet of galleys at Herradura Bay, it was said in 1563 that 'the construction of new ships could only partly compensate for the losses of the Spanish fleet'. This, moreover, was at a period of rapidly escalating prices; a vessel of 500 tons that would have cost 4,000 ducats in the time of Charles V would cost 15,000 by 1612, according to Tome Cano in his *Arte de Navegar*. So, in sum, it is scarcely surprising that not all the vessels assembled by Philip for his Armada were perfect for all eventualities, foreseen and unforeseen. The last word, however, must go to Don Garcia of Toledo, who as General de la Mar wrote to Philip's ambassador in Genoa in 1564: 'It is a fact clearly established that all sea expeditions during winter are a complete waste of money . . . We shall squander money without the least return as has already happened on many occasions and will happen again until the end of time if anything is to happen at this time of year.' Who was to foresee that 1588 was, in its way, to be all winter?

Sources Consulted for Chapter 4

Arnold, J.B., and Weddle, R.S., *The Nautical Archaeology of Padre Island*, London, 1978

Bankston, J., *Nautical Instruction, 1587*, Arizona, 1986

Braudel, F., *The Mediterranean and the Mediterranean World in the Age of Philip II*, London, 1982

Dudsus, A., and Henriot, E., *Dictionary of Ship Types*, London, 1986

Flanagan, L., Martin, C., and Stenuit, R., *Tresors de l'Armada*, Brussels, 1985

Kemp, P., *The Oxford Companion to Ships and the Sea*, London, 1976

Lewis, M., *The Spanish Armada*, London, 1960

McKee, A., *From Merciless Invaders*, London, 1987

Martin, C., *Full Fathom Five*, London, 1987

Martin, C., 'La Trinidad Valencera: an Armada invasion transport lost off Donegal', *International J. Nautical Archeol.*, 8(1) 1979

Rule, M., *The Mary Rose*, London, 1982

Stenuit, R., *Treasures of the Armada*, London, 1974

The Ships and their Equipment

4.1 ANCHOR, Iron
1280mm l
Iron anchor, end of shank damaged; would have measured 2200mm from fluke to fluke; one fluke badly damaged
Girona

4.2 ANCHOR-RING, Iron and Concretion
710mm l
Large circular block of concretion over iron ring, approximately 480mm d, with 3 projections
La Trinidad Valencera

4.3 SINGLE BLOCK, Wood
650mm h
Large wooden single block, sheave 290mm d on wooden pin, scored for rope of 56mm d; score on outside continues into two holes at top, of 51mm d. Badly riddled with Toredo worm
La Trinidad Valencera

4.4 SINGLE BLOCK, Wood
225mm h
Smaller wooden single block, sheave
63mm d, scored for rope of 25mm
d, on surviving wooden pin. Score
on outside continues into two holes
at top of 20mm d in which traces of
rope survive
La Trinidad Valencera

4.5 SINGLE BLOCK, Wood
150mm l
Small oval block of wood, not
scored; sheave and pin both missing
La Trinidad Valencera

4.6 DOUBLE BLOCK, Wood and Iron
400mm l
Rectangular block with rounded
corners, 110mm w by 85mm t, with
two wooden sheaves one above the
other, each 105mm d, each scored.
One end retains rectangular-
sectioned iron strap, 60mm wide,
with possible traces of hook
La Trinidad Valencera

4.7 SINGLE BLOCK, Wood and Iron
309mm l
Oblong block with single sheave
95mm d, 24mm t, originally rotating
on iron pin; traces of iron hooks or
fasteners at both ends. An additional
hole at each end, one 33mm d, one
20mm d
La Trinidad Valencera

4.8 COMPOSITE SHEAVE, Wood and Iron
545mm d
2 pieces, approximately half, of large
composite (4-piece) wooden sheave,
joined with tenon and strengthened
with 2 iron bolts 21mm d and now
210mm l; central perforation 101mm
d. Scored on perimeter, 70mm t
La Trinidad Valencera

4.9 COAK, Bronze
64mm w
Square coak, or bearing for block,
with slightly tapering sides; central
perforation 35mm d
La Trinidad Valencera

4.10 COAK, Bronze
60mm w
As above; central perforation
22mm d
La Trinidad Valencera

4.11 COAK, Bronze
37mm w
As above; central perforation 18mm
d; one of four this size from
the *Girona*
Girona

4.12 COAK, Bronze
42mm w
As above; central perforation 17mm
d; one of 6 this size from the *Girona*
Girona

4.13 COAK, Bronze
58mm w
As above; central perforation 25mm
d; one of 3 this size from the *Girona*
Girona

4.14 COAK, Bronze
63mm w
As above; central perforation 24mm
d; one of 2 this size from the *Girona*
Girona

4.15 COAK, Bronze
74mm w
As above; central perforation 29mm
d; one of 7 this size from the *Girona*
Girona

4.16 COAK, Bronze
84mm w
As above; central perforation 33mm
d; one of 5 this size from the *Girona*
Girona

4.17 COAK, Bronze
110mm w
As above; central perforation 43mm
d; the largest from the *Girona*
Girona

4.18 HEART, Wood
344mm l
Roughly pear-shaped block of wood,
scored on the perimeter for a rope
approximately 80mm in diameter; a
large quadrangular hole, 180mm h,
passes through the lower part to
receive another rope/ropes
La Trinidad Valencera

4.19 HEART, Wood
220mm l
As above, but scored for a rope
some 38mm d; part of the scoring
seems to have been made by
burning. The quadrangular opening
is 82mm h
La Trinidad Valencera

4.20 HEART, Wood
183mm l
As above, but scored for a rope of
some 40mm d; the opening is 60mm
h. A hole 7mm d has been pierced
in the upper part, across the long
axis, and simple geometric patterns
have been scratched on one face
La Trinidad Valencera

4.21 HEART, Wood
136mm l
As above, but better finished and
with a circular perforation of 20mm
d and another of 6mm d at narrow
end; scored for a rope of
approximately 26mm d
La Trinidad Valencera

4.22 EUPHROE, Wood
205mm l
Flat pear-shaped piece of wood,
22mm t, with 5 holes in a line along
the long axis, each 19mm d; for
making crow's feet
La Trinidad Valencera

4.23 SHACKLE, Iron
135mm l
U-shaped piece of round-sectioned
wrought iron, with a perforated lug
at each end through which is passed
a bar of iron, 25mm d and 170mm l
Girona

4.24 SHACKLE, Iron
103mm l
As above but smaller and lacking the
bar through the lugs
Girona

4.25 EYE-BOLT, Iron
310mm l
Threaded bar of iron 25mm d,
encased in iron sleeve; 'eye' missing
Girona

4.26 EYE-BOLT, Iron
90mm l
Evidently the eye from an eye-bolt
consisting of a loop of iron 10mm t
Girona

4.27 CHAINS, Iron in concretion
515mm l; 165mm w
At least 5 links of iron chain, 15mm
thick and each link 310mm l, totally
encased in concretion
La Trinidad Valencera

4.28 ROPE, Hemp
30mm d
Short section of rope consisting of
three left-hand laid strands laid
right-handed
La Trinidad Valencera

4.29 ANCHOR-CABLE, Hemp
130mm d
Over 2 metres of cable composed of
four strands, each laid right-handed,
all laid left-handed on a right-hand
laid heart rope
La Trinidad Valencera

**4.30 LANTERN, Wood and
LANTERN PEGS**
168mm d
Round lid of lantern, originally with
carrying strap of leather attached by
2 surviving wooden pegs, turned
from a single block. The lower rim
has 5 slots to take the sides of the
lantern, which were held in place by
wooden dowels
La Trinidad Valencera

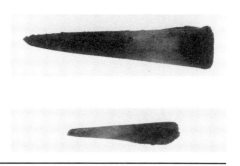

4.31 LANTERN, Wood
230mm d
Domed wooden lid carved from a
single block with central hole on
top; 3 side-pieces survive, varying
between 45 and 60mm w, grooved
along the edges to receive glass or
horn; held in place by peg-ends
which fit in holes provided in the
top and the 230mm d wooden base
La Trinidad Valencera

4.32 BANNER OR PENNANT, Wool
1100mm l
Part of a banner or pennant in dark red wool to which is applied, on the left, an eagle-like figure in yellow/tan wool; on the right is another appliqué motif, possibly the tail of a creature. The straight top-edge of the banner can be seen at top right
La Trinidad Valencera

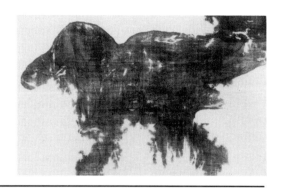

4.33 BOATSWAIN'S PIPE, Silver
70mm+l; 19.20+g
Three fragments of a boatswain's pipe, the mouth-piece and part of the decoration deficient; the surviving fragments include the sounding-chamber
Girona

4.34 SHEET, Lead
510mm l; 8 kg
Rectangular sheet of lead approximately 10mm t, with rounded corners. At each end is a square punched hole for attachment
Girona

4.35 SHEET, Lead
570mm l; 12 kg
As above but with 4 quadrangular perforations
Girona

4.36 WHEEL-FELLOE, Wood
502mm l
One out of five felloes of a wooden wheel, originally some 450mm d; this section has 2 slots for spokes, one of which survives, and in each end is a hole to receive a connecting peg
La Trinidad Valencera

4.37 ROLL OF SHEETING, Lead
383mm w; 5.4kg
Sheet lead, approximately 0.5mm
thick, in a roll
La Trinidad Valencera

4.38 CLAW-HAMMER, Iron and Wood
220mm l
Iron claw-hammer of square section,
50 x 50mm; portion of wooden
handle survives
La Trinidad Valencera

4.39 SPALL-HAMMER, Iron and Wood
220mm l
Iron spall-hammer of square section,
50 x 50mm at head end; spall tapers
to 15 x 15mm. Portion of wooden
handle survives
La Trinidad Valencera

4.40 MALLET, Wood
198mm l
Basically square-sectioned, but with
every angle chamfered to give
hexagonal section; in the socket,
20mm d, a small portion of handle
survives
La Trinidad Valencera

4.41 MALLET, Wood
230mm l
Rectangular-sectioned head, 80 x
45mm on surviving shaft of 20mm d
La Trinidad Valencera

4.42 BELLOWS, Wood
445mm l
Back and front plates of pair of
bellows: back-plate pear-shaped with
straight-sided handle and a
perforated nozzle at the other end;
hole 37mm d at top; front-plate
similar, decorated with concentric
circles; had been connected at
nozzle-end with 3 iron nails
La Trinidad Valencera

4.43 HEDDLE, Wood
465mm l
Blade formed from a single piece of
wood with 13 slots, approximately
242mm l, varying in width from 5 to
9mm. Each slat has a central 5mm
perforation
La Trinidad Valencera

4.44 WEAVER'S COMB, Wood
86mm w
Formed from a single piece of wood,
originally with 14 teeth, each 40mm
l, of which 5 survive
La Trinidad Valencera

4.45 BUCKET, Copper
210mm h
Formed of sheet copper with
circular bottom, approximately
220mm d. Reinforcement strap of
sub-circular bar rivetted to rim and
providing loops to receive the swan-
necks of the semicircular handle.
Badly squashed
La Trinidad Valencera

4.46 BUCKET, Copper
365mm w
As above, but more damaged and
has reinforced foot-ring
La Trinidad Valencera

4.47 WHISK OR BRUSH, Straw
345mm l
A simple bunch of straw, tied at the
middle with a light straw rope,
which is then bound tightly around
to form a handle
La Trinidad Valencera

4.48 BEARING(?), Wood
176mm l
Rectangular block of wood, 70mm
thick, with a semicircular hollow,
42mm in diameter, cut in the top.
On either side of the hollow a hole,
20mm in diameter, has been bored
right through the block, suggesting
that this block may have been one of
a pair joined together by dowels or
bolts. On the bottom are two further
rectangular slots, about 12 x 9mm
La Trinidad Valencera

4.49 WEDGE, Wood
144mm l
Wedge of wood cut radially from the
tree, 110mm wide and diminishing
from 50mm thick at the back to
9mm at the front
La Trinidad Valencera

4.50 NAIL/FASTENER, Iron
215mm l
Square-sectioned nail or fastener
15mm t at top, with turned-over
head
Girona

4.51 SHEAVE, Wood and bronze
210mm d
Circular wooden sheave, 45mm t,
scored for rope of 30mm d; central
coak, 65mm w with central
perforation of 29mm d, is still in
position; no pin
La Trinidad Valencera

4.52 SHEAVE, Wood
120mm d
Circular wooden sheave 30mm t,
scored for rope; Central setting for
bronze coak 40mm w, with circular
hole on other side 21mm d
La Trinidad Valencera

4.53 CAULKING HAMMER (?), Wood
250mm l
Cylindrical block of wood – now
slightly oval – gently curved along
long axis. Remains of wooden
handle 15mm d still in position.
Each end is rebated for
approximately 25mm and has tack-
holes to hold a covering, e.g. of
leather
La Trinidad Valencera

4.54 AWL, Wood and steel
90mm l
Turned wooden handle with
spherical terminal, 15mm d, with
portion of steel awl still in position
La Trinidad Valencera

CHAPTER 5
Navigation

By and large until the end of the fifteenth century most navigation was coastal by way of known landmarks in daylight. Previously, the Vikings, for example, were making regular trips backwards and forwards between Scandinavia and Iceland or Greenland, with only the wind, ocean currents, the sun and the stars to guide them; but it was not until the time of Columbus that sailing out into the open sea became usual. The search for 'New Worlds' and frequent journeys across the Atlantic led to the need for reliable means of navigation.

Essentially two developments were necessary; on the one hand, a convenient means of recording the cumulative experience of navigators and, on the other, instruments to enable each successive navigator to key into this recorded experience and to make his own contributions to it. One navigational aid that had existed for the benefit of coastal navigators was the sounding lead. By means of this, not only could the depth of water be measured, but by filling a depression in the base of the lead with tallow, to which samples of the sea-bed would adhere, a skilled coastal navigator could make more informed guesses as to his position. If, for example, the seabed sample showed alluvial mud as well as, or instead of, sand, he could reckon that he was near a river-mouth. The two sounding leads from the *Girona* (Cat 5.9–5.10) have such depressions and such leads are still in use today. For deep-sea soundings, of perhaps 100 fathoms (200m), the heavier lead was used.

The recording of the cumulative experience of navigators came first in the form of portolanos, which were little more than lists of coastal features in sequence, sometimes with additional information about shoals and sandbanks. Eventually an attempt was made to express this information graphically, as a form of early chart. Often the portolan chart showed little more than the outline of the seacoast, with the names of the coastal cities and ports, the headlands and promontories; but it was lavishly decorated with the flags and banners of those towns, and elaborate compass roses with a series of rhumb lines, largely decorative, extending from them; in total these would cover virtually the entire surface of the goatskin or sheepskin on which the chart was drawn. There were two inherent flaws in early charts: in the first place the accurate measuring of distances at sea was not perfected; in the second the difficulty of representing a curved surface on a flat sheet had not been overcome. It was Mercator, the Flemish geographer, who first attempted to solve this second problem. His projection, by presenting the parallels of latitude and the meridians of longitude as crossing one another at right angles, made possible the meaningful use of the rhumb lines as straight lines which could be used as actual ships' courses. Although Mercator introduced his projection as early as 1569, it was not until some 40 years after his death in 1594 that the sea-chart based on it was in common use.

To the modern eye these early charts show their inaccuracies very clearly; the shape of Ireland, for example, in many of them has not taken on the familiar appearance. To the smoothing-out on charts of the west coast of Ireland and the contraction, if not virtual disappearance, of Erris Head, has been attributed some, at least, of the blame for so many Spanish ships coming to grief on that coast. Baptista Boazio's famous map, as opposed to sea-chart, of 1599, shares with the charts the smoothing of the Irish west coast. One of the few examples that does indicate the seaward thrust of Erris Head to something approaching the modern representation is a much-folded 'pocket' chart, attributed to Sir Francis Drake, who had served in Irish waters, as naval commander when Sir John Norris extirpated the population of Rathlin Island in 1575. This, remarkably, is one of the few surviving charts to have degrees of latitude marked. Such a chart, of course, would have been essential for the person preparing the sailing directions for the returning Armada, and desirable, at least, for the other pilots.

Even the name 'Erris Head' is rarely to be identified among the features of the west coast of Ireland; one of the few examples is on a chart of 1544 by Baptista Agnese, where it appears as 'c. deros'. In fact the recognisable coastal features are often extremely difficult to reconcile with known name-forms, ancient or modern. The most consistently and frequently cited are Aranmore, Teelin and Killybegs in Co. Donegal; Sligo, in Co. Sligo; Burrishoole, the Clew Bay islands, Inishbofin and Slyne Head, in Co. Mayo; Galway and the Aran Islands in Co. Galway; Loop Head, in Co. Clare; Limerick, at the mouth of the Shannon; Tralee, the Blaskets and Dingle, in Co. Kerry; and Bear Haven and Cape Clear in Co. Cork. Scattered between these are variable, but for the most part unidentifiable, other names, including, quite frequently, the totally mythical 'Brazill'. The incidence of named, and therefore presumably known, places does not indicate a close familiarity with the coast, at least on the part of the chart-makers.

Not surprisingly no actual charts have survived on any of the wreck-sites, although a small portion of print, bound into the leather cover of a book, was recovered from the wreck of the *Mary Rose*; this suggests that, given the right circumstances, it is not totally impossible. However, among the material recovered from the *Girona*, there are five pairs of bronze or brass navigational dividers (Cat 5.5–5.8) and from *La Trinidad Valencera* another, extremely elegant pair, perfectly preserved (Cat 5.4). These imply the existence of charts and any used with them would surely bear the marks, even with the most gentle-fingered of navigators, of working on a seldom still ship.

Unsatisfactory though the existing charts may have been, in order to use them at all, two pieces of equipment were necessary, both of which were in existence in the sixteenth century: one device to show direction, and another to indicate how far to sail once the required direction has been achieved. The use of both is clearly demonstrated in the sailing instructions Medina Sidonia issued to the fleet once he was reconciled to the fact that the Armada had failed in its objective. The mariners' magnetic compass, although possibly in existence since the thirteenth century, had only achieved common use by the sixteenth. Basically it consisted of a magnetised needle, pivoting freely on a pin, with a card attached to it. While the effects of magnetic variation were not totally, or universally, appreciated, the nature of the card, with its necessarily rather imprecise divisions, tended to mitigate the effects. Instead of being divided into 360 degrees, the card was calibrated in cardinal points of north, south, east and west, then into half-cardinals and finally into 32 points; this meant that the most precise course feasible was only to 11.25°. Since annual change of variation is only about ten minutes, its effects would be minimal. Such a compass would have been part of the navigational equipment of every ship in the Armada and the base of one has survived from *La Trinidad Valencera* (Cat 5.1). A more complete one, still in its little box and mounted on gimbals, was recovered from the English *Mary Rose*. A portrait of Sir Edward Fiennes, an Elizabethan admiral, shows him holding a similar compass.

The compass having indicated the direction in which to sail, what was then needed was something to show how far to sail on a given course. Two gadgets were developed to fulfil this role: the astrolabe and the cross-staff. Both were used to measure the altitude of either the sun or a star – in the northern hemisphere usually the Pole Star. Each had its own merits and demerits. The astrolabe (of which two incomplete specimens survive from the *Girona* (Cat 5.2–5.3) as well as an apparently unfinished example, presumed to be from an Armada ship, from near Valentia Island) consists of a massive ring of bronze or brass, heavier at the bottom. This ring is graduated or calibrated around the edge, marks which, needless to say, have not survived on either example from the *Girona*, because of conditions on the site. At the centre is pivoted a sight-rule or alidade. The instrument was suspended by the suspension ring attached to the top and the alidade moved about its axis until the sun or star could be sighted along it and the altitude read off the ring's calibrations. The latitude at which the ship was situated could then be calculated. It was, of course, extremely difficult to obtain accurate readings from an astrolabe on the deck of a ship, particularly if the weather was at all boisterous.

The cross-staff, of which no examples, or even recognisable parts, have so far been recovered from any Armada wrecks, was in some respects superior to the astrolabe. It consisted of a square-sectioned staff, about three feet long, fitted with a sliding cross-piece or transom at right angles to it, which was held in place with a set screw. The staff was held to the navigator's eye, while the upper and lower ends of the cross-piece were made to coincide with the sun, or the star, being observed, with the horizon vertically beneath it. The point where the cross-piece intersects with the calibrated staff is noted and this value converted into degrees and minutes of latitude by reference to a set of tables. The cross-staff was easier to use on the moving deck of a ship and, because it was on a larger scale, it was possible to get a more accurate reading. If, however, the observed body was very high in the sky and the angle therefore quite large, it was difficult to scan it. It is not totally surprising that a cross-staff has not been recovered yet because of its relatively flimsy construction; the presence of a cross-staff on board one of the Padre Island wrecks, Texas, was inferred from the discovery of a brass set screw.

Longitude remained a problem until the eighteenth century because of the difficulties of measuring time sufficiently accurately at sea. The 'clocks from Lisbon' referred to in de Palacio's book remain a mystery and certainly any clocks available in the sixteenth century would not have been sufficiently accurate for establishing longitude with any confidence. 'Hour-glasses from Venice' are also mentioned; the Venetian source may be the glass-factories of Murano. The first mechanical time-keeping device for use at sea did not appear until after the establishment of a 'Board of Longitude' in 1714, which offered a prize for the development of a suitable instrument. It was not until 1764 that such a machine was perfected by John Harrison, and even then he had to wait until 1773 to receive all of his prize.

The sailing instructions issued by Medina Sidonia had read:

The course that is to be followed first is to the north-north-east, up to the latitude of 61.5 degrees; you will take great care lest you fall upon the Island of Ireland, for fear of the harm that may befall you on that coast. Then parting from these islands and rounding the Cape in 61.5 degrees you will run west-south-west until you are in latitude 58 degrees and then southwest until 53 degrees; then south-south-east to Cape Finisterre and so you will procure your entrance into Corunna.

These instructions, relying only on the compass and the astrolabe or cross-staff, would have taken the Armada up north of the Shetlands, then down to a point west of the Hebrides; reaching an area well to the west of Ireland, slightly south of Galway, it could then head straight home, without any reliance on faulty charts. It worked for Medina Sidonia himself in the 1,000 ton *San Martin*, the *capitana general*, flagship of the fleet, guiding him and his crew back to port, with the main body of the fleet, on 21 September – the very day the *Santa Maria de la Rosa* sank in Blasket Sound.

One important navigational aid which we tend to take for granted was totally lacking along the west coast of Ireland in 1588. This was the lighthouse. That at Alexandria, built in the third century BC, had been noted as one of the wonders of the Ancient World; the Romans had built lighthouses at, for example, Dover, in the first or second century AD, and, interestingly enough (for the Armada story), at La Coruna. However, the first lighthouses in Ireland were not built until after 1665, in response to the number of wrecks that were being sustained. These were private lighthouses, by patent granted to Sir Robert Reading; on the east coast they were situated at Howth, Co. Dublin, and on one of the Copeland Islands off Co. Down; on the south coast, at the Old Head of Kinsale, Co. Cork; the sole example to the west was on Loop Head, Co. Clare, at the extreme end of the Shannon mouth, on the north side of the river. Even these few were relatively humble constructions, of but a single storey, containing living accommodation for the keeper and with a small platform on the roof from which the light was provided by an open peat fire. Whether the existence of lighthouses, even if more providently sited, would have been a great boon to the Spanish fleet in the circumstances is open to grave doubt.

That navigation was taken extremely seriously by the Spanish and, indeed, the Portuguese, (one of whose Royal Princes is still known to history as 'Henry the Navigator') is shown by a forward-looking act of the *Casa de Contratacion*; this body, set up in 1503 to control and encourage the trade with the Indies, established as early as 1508 a hydrographic bureau and school of navigation. The first director, or Pilot Major, was no less a person than Amerigo Vespucci, the Florentine merchant-adventurer who at least gave his name to America, even if his claims to have been the first to discover it were exaggerated. One of his successors in office was Sebastian Cabot, son of the more famous Giovanni, or John, Cabot, who discovered Newfoundland in 1497; he claimed it on behalf of Henry VII of England and for this which was awarded a prize of ten pounds. The duties of the Pilot Majors included not only teaching would-be pilots navigation, but also examining and issuing licences to those who satisfied them with their knowledge. One of the other functions of the bureau was to keep up-to-date an official map of the world, by collating information obtained from returning navigators. The roles of teacher and examiner were separated in 1552 and the instructor was required to teach the use of compass, astrolabe and cross-staff, as well as the use of charts in plotting the ship's position. The *Casa* also issued astrolabes and cross-staffs, each with an official mark, to ensure that they were accurate; astrolabes recovered from the Padre Island, Texas, wreck, appear to bear this mark of approval. Despite certain apparent shortcomings, the *Casa*'s bureau and school won the admiration even of Englishmen; one such was Richard Hakluyt, who was one of the many persons of greater or lesser learning to publish treatises on navigation in the sixteenth century. Further works on navigation were produced by Cortes in 1551 and by de Medina in 1552. This last retained the astronomical system of Ptolemy, despite the publication in 1543 of the revolutionary work of the Polish astronomer, Copernicus. The famous English edition of Wagenaer's sea-atlas *The Mariner's Mirror* was published, coincidently, in 1588. Its well-known title page illustrates all the basic navigational equipment in use at the time. The work by Diego Garcia de Palacio, *Instrucion Nauthica*, the first part of which deals with navigation, was published in Mexico in 1587 and Richard Hakluyt's *Prinicipal Navigations* in 1589.

While some of the important work on navigation may have been for intellectual satisfaction, as a typical example of the enquiring mind of Renaissance Man, there is no doubt that political and commercial considerations were paramount. The reason the *Casa de Contratacion* established its school was to help ensure that the treasure-laden galleons, or as many as possible of them, returned safely from the New World, bringing wealth to Spain. Not only was there the fear that some of the galleons might lose their way, but also that other parties, knowing where the way normally was, might lie in wait there for ships on course and capture the treasure. There was, therefore, a certain element of secrecy about the trade-routes to the New World. As Francisco Mexia reported from Seville in 1553, 'Many French Basques are coming here claiming to be from Biscay. They go in the fleets, pretending to be loyal vassals of Your Majesty, and they later abuse their knowledge by becoming corsairs.' Two years later it was discovered that a Frenchman, Guiller Hamel, had deceitfully signed on as a gunner on a ship loading at Cadiz; the report stated: 'They say he is also a cosmographer and that he intends to learn all the ports of the Indies and the navigation.' Industrial or commercial espionage is nothing new.

Sources Consulted for Chapter 5

Arnold, J.B., and Weddle, R.S., *The Nautical Archaeology of Padre Island*, London, 1978

Bankston, J., *Nautical Instruction, 1587*, Arizona, 1986

Fallon, N., *The Armada in Ireland*, London, 1978

Flanagan, L., Martin, C., and Stenuit, R., *Tresors de l'Armada*, Brussels, 1985

Hague, D.B., *Lighthouses, Colston Papers 23*, London, 1973

Kemp, P., *The Oxford Companion to Ships and the Sea*, London, 1976

Rule, M., *The Mary Rose*, London, 1982

Stenuit, R., *Treasures of the Armada*, London, 1974

Westropp, T.J., 'Early Italian Maps of Ireland from 1300 to 1600', *Proc. Roy. Irish Acad.*, 30 1913

Navigation

5.1 MARINER'S COMPASS, Wood and Steel
104mm d
Turned wooden circular base of
Mariner's compass, with central steel
pin (now bent) on which the card,
divided into 32 points, to which was
attached the magnetised needle,
would have pivoted
La Trinidad Valencera

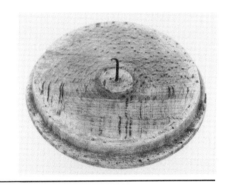

5.2 ASTROLABE, Bronze
189mm d
Circular bronze astrolabe with the
abraded remains of a suspension
loop at the top. The circle is divided
in four by cross-members which
meet in the centre to form a circular
perforated platform on which the
sight-rule or alidade, now missing,
would have pivoted. The lower
cross-member runs into a
semicircular weighted base which
helped keep the astrolabe vertical
when sights were being made. The
calibrations on the face of the ring
have been obliterated by sea-action
over nearly 400 years. The astrolabe
was used to measure the angle
between the Sun, or at night in the
Northern Hemisphere, the Pole
Star, and the horizon, from which
the ship's latitude could be
calculated
Girona

5.3 ASTROLABE, Bronze
1881mm d
As above except that the weighted
base is not semicircular and the
central platform not circular: each is
bordered by concave rather than
convex curves. This astrolabe has
broken into nine pieces
Girona

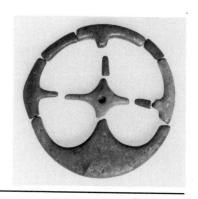

5.4 NAVIGATIONAL DIVIDERS, Bronze
120mm l
Pair of navigational dividers
consisting of two similar straight
legs, ending in a point at one end
and a G-shape at the other, at the
top of which they are held together
by a bronze rivet. The upper part of
each leg is decorated with motifs in
the form of the letter 'M'. These
dividers still function perfectly
La Trinidad Valencera

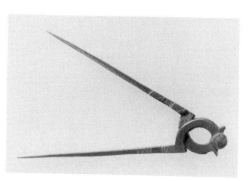

5.5 NAVIGATIONAL DIVIDERS, Bronze
133mm l
As above, but the legs, which
thicken at the top, are decorated
with a motif consisting of a single
'M' and are bent at the bottom; the
pivot no longer works
Girona

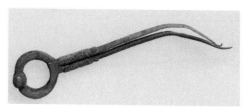

5.6 NAVIGATIONAL DIVIDERS, Bronze
98mm l
As above, but the legs are slightly
bent at the knee and the decoratiion
consists of simple linear motifs. The
pivot now functions through only
about half of its arc
Girona

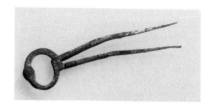

5.7 NAVIGATIONAL DIVIDERS, Bronze
107mm l
As above but plainer; part of of the
hinge is missing and some
concretion adheres to the top
Girona

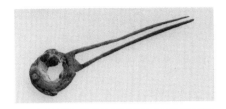

5.8 NAVIGATIONAL DIVIDERS, Bronze
102mm l
As above, of plain construction; the
top is embedded in concretion
Girona

5.9 SOUNDING LEAD, Lead
189mm l; 3.4kg
Long conical sounding lead with a
circular hole at the top to take the
line. In the base is a cupped
depression for filling with tallow to
take samples of the sea-bed
Girona

5.10 SOUNDING LEAD, Lead
216mm l; 5.1kg
As above but the hole for the line is
cross-shaped
Girona

CHAPTER 6
The Ordnance

When it sailed from Lisbon the Armada's 130 ships were carrying, between them, 2,431 guns of all sizes and sorts, 1,497 of bronze, the rest of iron. One, *La Florencia*, of the Squadron of Portugal, at 961 tons, carried an apparently amazing total of 52 guns; some of the very small pinnaces carried none at all. The assembling of such a body of ordnance was a most commendable achievement on the part of Medina Sidonia, but an achievement that, as we shall see, involved scraping the barrel and making use of pieces that were out-dated or hastily fashioned to meet requirements. As always in these circumstances, there were all too many fully prepared to cash in and provide sub-standard articles.

Although gunpowder had been in common military use for some 200 years (traditionally the first use of guns at sea was in 1336 in an attack on Antwerp), the sixteenth century saw the culmination of a slow evolution in gun-design that was to remain, for some time, relatively unchanged. The evolution of guns took its course in rather a haphazard way; each gun was so much of an individual that not only did it belong, in the loosest possible fashion, to a named type, but it actually enjoyed a specific name of its own, a sort of nick-name, by which it was identified. In England in 1475, for example, the Master of the Ordnance, John Sturgeon, delivered to store at Calais a consignment of guns which included 'a grete bastard gonne and her chambre called the Messenger'; the term 'bastard' alone suggests that the gun in question was not directly assignable to any recognised gun-type. The results of this haphazard development were, of course, likely to cause great difficulty to all gunners and all Masters of Ordnance, whatever nationality; the lack of standardisation caused difficulties with the supply of shot, for example, if each gun required shot of a different size or calibre. It was Charles I, King of Castile, Leon, Sicily and Aragon – that is, of Spain and, as Charles V, Emperor of Germany and the Low Countries – who decreed, in 1544, that there should be only seven models of ordnance manufactured for, and used by, the armies of the Empire, in an effort to resolve this problem. There is little evidence to suggest that his decree brought immediate success, and a great deal of evidence to suggest that it did not.

6.8 Swivel Gun, bronze and iron. Short cylindrical barrel of breech-loading swivel gun of 90mm calibre from *La Trinidad Valencera*. The trunnions are located 598mm from the muzzle and there are two lugs at the breech. The trunnions still retain the cast-iron Y-shaped support and the lugs the cast-iron trail. The gun is loaded and the barrel bears the weight-mark '1125'

8.13 and 8.14 Pestle and Mortar, bronze, from *La Trinidad Valencera*. A circular container of heavy bronze, with a slight foot at the base and a rounded interior bottom. Four lugs are fitted at the four quarters on the outside, each with three crests. The accompanying pestle has a central knop and expands gently from the centre to end in two pear shapes

The multiplicity of gun-types is revealed by the number of names in use, often revealing the mixed national origins of gunnery and of certain gun-types; in sixteenth-century England, for example, a selection of such names includes base, basilisk, bombard, culverin, perier, drake, falcon, minion, saker, passavolante, serpentine, as well as cannons and demi-cannons. Many of these terms are obviously derived from, or instantly translatable into, other languages: Spanish 'canon' is instantly recognisable as 'cannon', 'culebrina' as 'culverin', 'sacre' as 'saker'. What is, perhaps, a little surprising is the number of gun-names that relate to birds: for example, falcon, saker, (but not drake, it relates to 'dragon'); snakes: for example, culverin or serpentine; or even, more surprisingly still, to a lover: for example, minion.

To add to the complexity, in addition to types of gun, which usually relate to size of shot and length of range, there were in the sixteenth century three main ways of making pieces of ordnance and two main materials from which they were made. The two materials, of course, were iron and bronze. The iron guns could be of wrought iron or cast iron. Wrought iron examples could be made by forming a large tube from a single plate of wrought iron and forge-welding it along the seam, then hot-shrinking a series of collars and hoops onto the barrel to create a strong, gas-tight tube. Alternatively a tube or cylinder could be fashioned by welding together strips or bars of wrought iron and then strengthening this by means of hot-shrunk collars or sleeves. Such guns of wrought iron had been in use on the *Mary Rose* when she sank in 1545 and were in use on the wrecks of 1554 at Padre Island in the Texas Gulf. They were, of necessity, breech-loaders. Often the difficulty of avoiding the escape of gas at the breech caused these guns to be extremely dangerous in operation.

Before Armada sites were excavated, wrought iron guns were reckoned so antiquated for the period that their appearance on any of the ships was deemed unthinkable; even on the *Mary Rose* it had been seriously considered that the first wrought iron guns found, albeit fully loaded and ready for action, had come from the hold where they had been used as ballast (unlikely though this explanation might seem). Thus, when two such guns, each about 2m long with bores of 80 to 90mm, were found on the wreck-site of *El Gran Grifon* at Fair Isle, together with a breech-block of the right type but the wrong size (indicating that at least three of these weapons, more obsolete than obsolescent, were on board), it came as a great surprise and a certain indication that Medina Sidonia really had to scrape the barrel in order to arm the Armada. In addition to these guns, probably corresponding to the description of 'large esmerils', four other, smaller, iron breech-blocks were found, belonging to the kind of swivel-gun, or verso, so well known from the Padre Island wrecks. Even though *El Gran Grifon* was an urca, and as such, almost by definition, non-combatant, she was, after all, the flagship of the squadron, so the fact that at least five of her complement of thirty-eight guns were of this construction really was surprising. As de Palacio says: 'In my opinion, of the iron pieces, only the cast iron ones ought to be used for anything, and being careful with them, they may be usefully employed and are safe.' No wrought iron guns have so far been found on any of the Irish wrecks, possibly because those ships excavated were of larger size and were considered as front-line fighting ships.

Guns of cast iron, on the other hand, were almost an innovation at the time of the Armada, to the extent that the proportion of these, as opposed to bronze, guns being made continued to rise throughout the seventeenth century. Eventually, by the end of the eighteenth century, the former had virtually replaced the latter material.

So far six cast iron guns have been recorded on Armada wreck-sites. Only one is connected with an Irish wreck, that is, the iron falcon removed from the *Duquesa Santa Ana* by Don Alonso de Leiva when she sank at Loughros More, Co. Donegal and used by him to defend his small fortification of Kiltoorish Lake, near to the wreck-site. This was a quite plain piece, 2.35m long with a bore of some 15mm. Unfortunately within days, literally, of Robert Stenuit's publishing the location of this piece, it was removed. The other five finds are all from *El Gran Grifon*. The first was a small saker, a badly eroded piece, some 2.70m long, with a bore of 75mm and a ball firmly wedged in its exposed barrel. Two others were more stubby, about 2m long and with bores of 100mm, probably quarter cannons, while the final two were of only 50mm calibre and only about 1.30m long, small guns that correspond to no standard category. These guns, fortunately, are all preserved in the Shetland Museum in Lerwick.

Since the bronze guns carried by the Armada outnumbered those of iron by nearly two to one and since they have a considerably greater chance of preservation than iron ones, it is not surprising that more of them have been recovered from Armada wrecks, especially those in Ireland. (On *El Gran Grifon* off Fair Isle, contrarily, the picture is totally the reverse: two bronze guns to five of iron.) Another useful fact about bronze guns is that they are more likely to be decorated and/or bear an indication of the maker and even the owner.

In the sixteenth century, there were bronze-foundries throughout Europe where bronze ordnance was cast: at Utrecht in Holland, Malines in Belgium, Parma and Venice in Italy, Malaga in Spain and, of course in England, mainly in London, to mention only a few. Many of the gun-founders achieved high reputations for their skills and the trade was, indeed, a highly-skilled calling. The difficulties of casting a cylinder of bronze, perhaps as much as 3m long, without cracks or flaws, and with an even thickness of metal all round the core, are considerable; all founders did not always succeed. A picture does exist of a sixteenth-century gun-foundry in the Low Countries. The casting mould stands upright in a deep pit, breech down; the molten metal is poured from the furnace into the gunhead – known as the 'gate' in a mould for other bronze objects – while a treadmill powers a machine for reaming out the bores. Interestingly the furnace is being fed with scrap metal, broken pieces of ordnance for the most part. Unless the scrap came from spoiled pieces in the same foundry, it must have been difficult to ensure the right mix of copper and tin to make the best gun-metal; too much tin and the metal becomes too hard and brittle. In the illustration, other craftsmen stand or sit at their work of cleaning up the surfaces and surface-features of guns that have already been cast. It is not surprising that a large pulley-block with two sheaves stands in the foreground; lifting a piece weighing three tons or so from the casting-pit would certainly require some mechanical assistance.

The guns recovered from Armada wrecks show a wide range of the products of the sixteenth-century gun-founders – from the very best to the worst. Among the very best certainly are to be numbered the large bronze siege-guns from *La Trinidad Valencera* (Cat 6.1–6.2). Each bears the inscription: *IOANES . MARICUS . A . LARA . FIERI . CURAVIT / OPUS . REMIGY . DE . HALUT / ANNO 1556* . which translates as 'Juan Manrique de Lara caused this to be made, the work of Remigy de Halut, 1556'. They also bear the Royal Arms of Philip II of Spain, as King of England – this as a consequence of his marriage to Mary Tudor in 1554 – as well as the name *PHILIPPUS REX*. Nearly 3m long, with a bore of 183mm, both are delicately decorated all over, with acanthus-leaf motifs at the muzzle and in front of the trunnions, and each has a pair of solid, cast dolphins for lifting it, and another similar dolphin forming the breech-ring. One is in markedly better condition than the other, as a result of being totally buried in sand.

We know from the manifest of *La Trinidad Valencera* that she was carrying three of these guns and the identifying weights for all three are given: 5316, 5160 and 5260. The first two recovered had their weights inscribed just above the escutcheons: 5316 and 5160; it was predicted that the third, weighing 5260, was on board. It was, in fact, found and raised in the spring of 1987, with, indisputably, the weight 5260 stamped on it.

Juan Manrique de Lara, who caused these magnificent guns to be made, was a well-known soldier and diplomat. Between 1551 and 1574, when he died, he was Captain-General of Artillery for the Kingdoms of Aragon and Castile and in 1556, when the guns were cast, he was serving as Captain-General of Artillery in the Army of Flanders. (He had actually also been responsible for securing Papal approval for the marriage of Philip and Mary in 1554, when he was serving as Imperial Ambassador in Rome, so he was a statesman as well as a soldier and administrator.)

The story of the foundry in Malines run by Remigy de Halut is an interesting one. Malines, or Mechelen, is a town not far from Brussels in what is now Belgium. There had existed here for many years a foundry, under the direction of Hans Poppenruyter, who had begun to achieve a reputation for the quality of his ordnance in the late fifteenth century, to the extent that Henry VIII of England became one of his best customers. In the first quarter of the sixteenth century, Henry bought from Poppenruyter some 144 pieces of ordnance, which included a fine order placed by his agent Spinelly in 1510 for 24 curtows, each averaging 4,000lb in weight, and 24 serpentines of 1,100lb. These were delivered and paid for in 1512. It was this foundry that cast Henry's famous set of guns known as 'The Twelve Apostles', a dozen large curtows weighing 5,600lb each. Unfortunately Henry later proved better at ordering than paying, so in 1526 the foundry stopped supplying him. Charles I of Spain had, however, selected Malines as his royal gun foundry and Poppenruyter his Founder Royal, which more than compensated for the loss of Henry as a customer.

In 1526, Poppenruyter had married Hedwige van den Nieuwenhuysen who proved an able assistant in the administration of the foundry, so much so that when Hans died in 1534, without legal heir other than his wife, she carried on with the running of the foundry. She found a suitable person to assist her in the business in Remigy de Halut, who in his youth had served in an artillery regiment, and in 1536 she also married him. In due course he was confirmed as Poppenruyter's successor as Founder Royal as well. De Halut cooperated in the attempts to standardise ordnance by laying down prescriptions for calibre, barrel-length, thickness of walls and total weight. He also introduced proof-firing at the foundry, whereby each piece, before delivery to the customer, was fired at the foundry with a heavier charge of fine-grained powder than would normally be used. This, then, was the manner in which Remigy de Halut was in a position to cast Philip's guns in 1556 in Malines, where the King had established his main ordnance depot for the Low Countries in 1550.

In fact the three guns now recovered from *La Trinidad Valencera* were part of a complete siege-train of 54 siege-guns, each averaging 5,500lbs, made by de Halut. At the time of Santa Cruz's feasability study for the Armada in 1586, these guns were scattered throughout the Empire: 12 in Sicily, 17 in Naples, another 25 at Cartagena, Malaga and Lisbon. From these outposts of Empire they were obviously recalled to serve in the Armada. Perhaps they were intended primarily to fulfil their true role of siege-guns during the invasion of England,but also, it would appear, to augment the armament of some of the ships, including *La Trinidad Valencera*.

Quite a number of other guns cast by Remigy de Halut survive. A saker, 2,773mm long and of 102mm bore, is in the Armouries of the Tower of London; bearing the Royal Arms of Philip II, again as King of England, with the date '1555', it is further evidence of his supply to Philip. Since this gun had been in Lee Castle in Lanarkshire for a number of years it is not impossible that it may have come from an Armada wreck. In the Museu de Artilharia in Lisbon is a handsome cannon made for the Duke of Braganza in Portugal, bearing his arms as well as his name. Another, earlier piece, made for Charles I of Spain, was destroyed in the disastrous fire at the Tower Armouries in 1841.

Three other pieces of ordnance recovered from *La Trinidad Valencera* probably were part of her original armament (Cat 6.3–6.5). The first of these is a medium-culverin, some 3,450mm in length and with a bore of 95mm. The decoration around the breech is exuberant, with swans, sea-creatures and flowering plants supporting a vase emitting flames; the flame-motif is continued on the chase of the gun. Beneath a foliated shield also on the chase appear the initials 'Z A', for Zuanne Alberghetti, a celebrated Venetian gun-founder.

The wealth and power of Venice developed from, and depended on, her sea-power. At the heart of this power was a remarkable institution; the Arsenal, the largest industrial complex in Europe. Established by 1100 in a water-basin between two marshy islands called Zemelle ('twins' in the Venetian dialect), it derived its name, ironically in view of Venice's precarious relationship with the Turks, from the Arabic *Dar Sina'a*, meaning 'house of industry'. The Arsenal developed prodigiously and even by 1480 provided covered accommodation for the simultaneous construction of 80 galleys, and shortly later 116. Not only galleys were made there, but also all their fittings and equipment: not only oars, masts, canvas and rope, but munitions as well. This, inevitably, had resulted in several bizarre accidents, on one occasion as a result of a spark from a horse's hoof. The entire enterprise was meticulously managed and quality-control was virtually invented in the Arsenal of Venice. The timber was specially selected and seasoned until it was iron-hard by soaking in sea-water.

It was in this context, therefore, that the celebrated Venetian family of gun-founders flourished. In addition to Zuanne, who made the *La Trinidad Valencera* gun, Hieronymo and Sigismondo were also active as gun-founders. Two very handsome identical bronze sakers, each 3.50m long, with bores of 91mm, by Zuanne were recovered from the wreck of a Venetian ship at Gnalic in the Adriatic. Both these guns were flamboyantly decorated, in true Italian Renaissance style, and each bore the date 'MDLXXXII' (1582). Examples of the work of Hieronymo, dated 'MDXXXXIII' (1583), and of Sigismondo, dated 'MDLXVIII' (1548) are in the Museo Storico Navale in Venice.

The other 'signed' gun from *La Trinidad Valencera* is a small demi-cannon, 3,220mm long and of 125mm bore. It is relatively undecorated, but bears the initials of another known Venetian gun-founder, Nicole de Conti. He is known to have worked with the Alberghetti family, but in the casting of works of art; some of their artistic work is still to be seen in the Piazza San Marco in Venice. The other probable Venetian gun is a saker, 2,880mm long, with a bore of 90mm; it is badly pitted and corroded and bears no maker's mark or date. It is, however, comparable to the Venetian work in style.

It is, perhaps, an interesting side-light on the difference in Renaissance attitudes in the north and in the south that while the Venetians cast guns and works of art, the Flemish cast guns and church-bells. A Poppenruyter bell still hangs in a church in East Scotland, at Kettins, near Dundee, bearing an inscription and the date '1519'.

The guns recovered from the *Girona* were a little disappointing; of the fifty guns she carried, only two and a fragment of a third survive, as well as breech-blocks for a fourth. This may be accounted for partly by her having had to jettison most of her armament at Killybegs to make room for as many men as possible or to some of her guns being salvaged by the McDonnells of Dunluce Castle, as local tradition would have it.

The two complete guns retrieved by Robert Stenuit were a half-saker (Cat 6.6) and an esmeril (Cat 6.9), neither in very good condition. The half-saker is short, as might be expected, 2,340mm long, with a bore of 76mm. The lifting dolphins have been almost totally eroded, leaving only their stumps. On the breech, however, is a still-legible, but barely so, coat of arms, evidently those of Philip II, surrounded by the collar of the Order of the Golden Fleece, as on the *La Trinidad Valencera* siege-guns. The esmeril, a small swivel-gun, to be mounted on an iron swivel on the gunwhale of the ship and used more as an anti-personnel weapon, is 1,630mm long, with a bore of a mere 52mm. This is a breech-loader, with a series of compatible and changeable bronze breech-blocks, which could be pre-loaded with powder in an attempt to increase the rate of fire. They were not popular with gunners because of a tendency to swivel round on firing and eliminate the wrong personnel. Breech-blocks of a larger size, for one of the larger esmeril-types, were also recovered.

The final *La Trinidad Valencera* gun was also a breech-loading swivel gun, but of larger calibre than the esmeril from the *Girona*, of 90mm bore (Cat 6.8). It is of bronze and retains not merely its iron swivel, which, however, no longer swivels, but also its tiller and a breech-block, complete with wedge (all items of iron), incorporating a back-sight, and a wad of chamois leather. It is still loaded. The final *Girona* gun, represented by a rather damaged piece of the muzzle, is a medium culverin, of 145mm bore (Cat 6.7). Despite the fact that it is skew-bored, like one of the guns from *El Gran Grifon*, it is more likely to have been broken in the crash of the wreck than to have exploded on firing.

This is not so with one of the guns recovered from the *Juliana*, wrecked at Streedagh. This is a saker, rather elegant, 3m long, with a bore of 90mm. It bears the date 'MDLXX' (1570), the figure of a bishop with a crozier and mitre, and the letter 'D' on the breech. It has also, sadly, a large hole near the muzzle where it appears to have blown out on firing. The other two guns raised were stubby pedreros, a mere 2m long with a bore of 145mm; one of these has also a 'D' at the breech, along with a representation of the Madonna and Child. The other, very similar, has a small floriated Cross just above the touch-hole.

The evidence of ordnance from Irish wrecks, therefore, is fairly wide-ranging, with representation of shorter-range guns, like the siege-guns for throwing heavy shot a short distance; some smaller calibre, longer-range guns, like *La Trinidad Valencera*'s medium culverin; and finally the very short-range anti-personnel weapons like the swivel-guns from *La Trinidad Valencera* and the *Girona*.

We have, in fact, far more than this. The site of *La Trinidad Valencera* has produced a great range of ancillary equipment. Not only are there gun-carriage wheels (Cat 6.38–6.39), apparently for both land-carriages and sea-carriages, but a host of other equipment as well. The gun-carriage wheels from *La Trinidad Valencera* and those observed at Streedagh are all large and spoked. Some most certainly – the larger ones – are the wheels of a land-carriage for one of the siege-guns, which would have been necessary in its primary role, besieging a walled town or castle. Some of the smaller wheels, however, must have been for sea-carriages, for other ordnance as well as the siege-guns. No solid wheels of relatively small diameter, such as those encountered on the *Mary Rose*, and which form an integral part of everyone's visual image of a sea-carriage, have been recovered. They have not even been observed on any Armada wreck, despite the fact that de Palacio prescribes that 'the carriage and wheels of this artillery are to be small, the wheels are to be solid and three palms [= 200mm] in diameter, and they ought not to be faulty, so that they roll better upon plank, are sufficient, and do not damage the deck.' It does seem surprising, therefore, that Armada ships, sailing from 'home' ports, should be equipped with more archaic gun-carriages than were in use in a colony.

Other gunners' equipment found included not only a barrel half-full of gunpowder and a charge of powder (Cat 6.13) which was successfully extracted from one of the *Girona* breech-blocks, but also a copper scoop for loading it, made, sensibly, of copper, to avoid the risk of sparks (Cat 6.14). Two linstocks were also recovered (Cat 6.15–6.16), each with its own application of humour in its design: one is in the form of a grotesque open-mouthed head, the slow match sticking out like a small tongue; the other in the form of a clenched fist, with an aperture along the fingers to contain the match. These, of course, were to protect the gunner when he was applying the lighted match to the priming powder in the gun's touch-hole (Cat 6.10).

A series of three shot-gauges (Cat 6.17–6.19), of wood but of different sizes, are an indication of how serious the problems of non-standardisation of shot and gun-calibres was likely to be; the gunner had to have a shot-gauge for each gun he tended, so he could ensure that any shot used was of the correct calibre. Equally important was the gunner's rule, which he used as a sort of ready-reckoner. The one from *La Trinidad Valencera* is of wood, with the calibrations, ranging from 50 to 120, still clearly legible (Cat 6.20). In point of fact, the rule recovered was remarkably inaccurate and must have alleviated the gunner's problems not one whit. Often, and increasingly in the seventeenth century, such rules were marked on the blades of gunners' stilettoes, particularly in Italy.

Large quantities of shot, both in cast iron and in stone, have been recovered from all the Armada wreck-sites so far investigated (Cat 6.21–6.33). There are examples of shot of the right calibre for most of the ordnance recovered, but in addition, inevitably, there is shot suitable for pieces which have not been recovered. One particularly rare find from *La Trinidad Valencera* is a piece of canister shot – a wooden hexagonal canister filled with lumps of iron – again intended as an anti-personnel weapon, fragmenting on impact (Cat 6.34). There has been a lively controversy about the inadequacies of Spanish shot-making techniques, as one possible reason for the apparent failure of Spanish guns and gunners to inflict significant damage on the English ships. The theory was that the Spanish shot was cooled too quickly in order to increase production-rates and the concentric rings shown in the section of the round of iron shot from the *Santa Maria de la Rosa* (Cat 6.29) is reckoned to demonstrate this artificially speeded cooling. It has, however, been suggested, to the contrary, that these rings were caused by advancing layers of corrosion penetrating from the surface.

Two other finds from *La Trinidad Valencera* helped to explain another, previously enigmatic, find. These are two sponge-heads, for cleaning and cooling the barrels of the guns between firings (Cat 6.36–6.37). With them, it is now realised, are to be associated the pieces of hairy goatskin recovered (Cat 6.40). In the receipt for ordnance and ancillary equipment loaded onto a ship about to voyage to the Americas in 1552, were included nineteen sheepskins for cleaning the guns; hairy goatskin is quite as applicable as sheepskin in this context.

In the manifest of *La Trinidad Valencera*, in addition to barrels of iron, there are references to ladles for making shot as well. None of these has so far been recovered. Other items that might be expected are gunners' quadrants, used for establishing the elevation of the gun required, and examples of other kinds of specialist shot in use, such as the '"Pelicans", "lanterns" of flints, nail-heads, and sheathing nails, bar-shot, goat-shot, and other inventions wherewith to give offense to the enemy', which de Palacio lists. It is possible, of course, that some of the powder-flasks found and even the buckets may have been used in connection with the ordnance.

Sources used for Chapter 6

Arnold, J.B., and Weddle, R.S., *The Nautical Archaeology of Padre Island*, London, 1978

Baker, R., 'Bronze Cannon-founders: comments upon Guilmartin 1974, 1982', *International J. Nautical Archaeol.*, (12.1) 1983

Bankston, J., *Nautical Instruction*, 1587, Arizona, 1986

Blackmore, H.L., *The Armouries of the Tower of London: The Ordnance*, London, 1976

Flanagan, L., Martin, C., and Stenuit, R., *Tresors de l'Armada*, Brussels, 1985

Guilmartin, J.F., 'The cannon of the Batavia and the Sacramento: early modern cannon-founding reconsidered', *International J. Nautical Archaeol.*, (11) 1982

Hutcheson, A., 'Notice of the Bell and other antiquities at the Church of Kettins, Forfarshire', *P. Soc. Antiq. of Scotland*, (28) 1894

Lewis, M., *Armada Guns*, London, 1961

Mann, Sir J., *Wallace Collection Catalogues: European Arms and Armour*, London, 1962

Martin, C., *Full Fathom Five*, London, 1975

McKee, A., *From Merciless Invaders*, London, 1986

Rule, M., *The Mary Rose*, London, 1982

Thubron, C., *The Venetians*, Amsterdam, 1981

Walker, B., *The Armada*, Amsterdam, 1982

The Ordnance

6.1 SIEGE GUN, Bronze

2900mm l

Large, slightly tapering, cylindrical barrel of muzzle-loading gun of a calibre of 183mm, with a breech-ring in the form of a dolphin and two dolphins for lifting. Two hefty trunnions of 127mm diameter are located 1340mm from the breech. A touch-hole, with fittings for a cover, of 12mm diameter, is located 370mm from the breech; acanthus-leaf decoration at the muzzle and forward of the trunnions. The breech-end bears the Arms of Philip II of Spain as King of England and the inscription *Philippus Rex*. The inscription on the breech-ring reads *IOANES. MARICUS. A. LARA. FIERI. CURAVIT / OPUS REMIGY. DE. HALUT / ANNO 1556* (Made on the instructions of Juan Manrique de Lara by Remigy de Halut in 1556) and the identifying weight inscribed on the gun reads '5316'. This was one of a Royal Siege-train of 54 pieces cast for Philip II, and one of three of these guns embarked on *La Trinidad Valencera*. In addition to prospective use for a siege of London it is likely they were used on board to augment the standard naval ordnance *La Trinidad Valencera*

6.2 SIEGE GUN, Bronze
2900mm l
As above, but in worse condition and with the recorded identifying weight of 5160
La Trinidad Valencera

6.3 MEDIUM CULVERIN, Bronze
3450mm l
A long and elegant barrel of a muzzle-loading gun of 95mm calibre, with trunnions located some 1570mm from the breech. The decoration round the breech consists of swans, sea-creatures and flowering plants supporting a flame-emitting vase; the flame-motif is continued on the chase of the barrel and the muzzle is adorned with entwined foliage. Beneath a foliated shield on

the chase appear the initials
'★Z★A★', for Zuanne Alberghetti, a
celebrated Venetian gun-founder.
This gun would have formed part of
the ship's original armament. It
bears the identifying weight '2529'
La Trinidad Valencera

6.4 SMALL DEMI-CANNON,
Bronze
3220mm l
A long, but stouter, barrel of a
muzzle-loading bronze gun, of some
125mm calibre, with trunnions
located some 1450mm from the
breech. Apart from a device with the
inscription 'SENPER' (presumably
for 'SEMPER' (always)) below
which appear the initials
'★N★D★C★', for Nicole de Conti,
another celebrated Venetian gun-
founder, the barrel is unornamented.
It bears the identifying weight
'2950'. This too would have formed
part of the ship's original armament
La Trinidad Valencera

6.5 SAKER, Bronze
2880mm l
A shorter cylindrical barrel of a
muzzle-loading gun of some 90mm
calibre, with trunnions located some
1290mm from the breech. This gun
is badly pitted and corroded and
apart from the remains of an
illegible coat of arms bears no
distinguishing marks. It too was
probably part of the ship's original
armament
La Trinidad Valencera

6.6 HALF-SAKER, Bronze
2340mm l
A short cylindrical barrel of a gun of
76mm calibre, with trunnions some

1100mm from the breech and the remains of lifting dolphins at the same place. This gun is quite badly corroded, but just legible on the chase are the Arms of Spain with the Chain of the Order of the Golden Fleece
Girona

6.7 MEDIUM CULVERIN, Bronze
520mm+l
The rather damaged muzzle portion of a breech-loading gun of 145mm calibre. Apart from two sets of double ridges at the muzzle this gun has no other features
Girona

6.8 SWIVEL GUN, Bronze and Iron.
1450mm l
Short cylindrical barrel of breech-loading swivel gun of 90mm calibre; trunnions are located 598mm from muzzle and there are two lugs at the breech. The trunnions still retain the cast-iron Y-shaped support and the lugs the cast-iron trail. The detachable iron breech-block has an open-loop handle; behind the breech-block, no longer detachable, is a cast iron wedge with a back-sight; behind this is a wad of chamois leather. The handle of the trail or tiller has been preserved for only 215mm of its original length. The gun is loaded and the barrel bears the weight-mark '1125' (see colour plate)
La Trinidad Valencera

6.9 ESMERIL, Bronze

1630mm l

Cast bronze barrel of breech-loading swivel gun of 52mm calibre; barrel circular at muzzle, hexagonal from there to breech, with trunnions located 104mm from muzzle. 60mm behind these the gun swells to accommodate the firing chamber, into which fits a (still) detachable breech block 330mm long. Neither the swivel nor the tiller survive, but there are rectangular slots and a circular hole at the rear of the breech, presumably to accommodate these fittings. This also bears the faintly legible Arms of Spain with the Chain of the Order of the Golden Fleece

Girona

6.10 TOUCH-HOLE COVER, Bronze

183mm l

Cast bronze lid for the touch-hole of one of the siege guns, with two perforated lugs admitting a pin 11mm diameter to hinge the cover over the touch-hole

La Trinidad Valencera

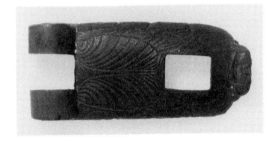

6.11 BREECH-BLOCK, Bronze

342mm l

Cylindrical breech-block with rectangular loop handle; at the front is a narrower projection to fit the breech end of the barrel, with a lug at the rear; the touch-hole is located to the rear and side of the handle; for use with the surviving swivel gun or an identical one

Girona

6.12 BREECH-BLOCK, Bronze
410mm l
As above but for a larger swivel gun
which has not been found
Girona

6.13 CHARGE, Gunpowder
212mm l
Charge of gunpowder extracted from
a breech-block of the Esmeril; about
half of its original section has been
abraded, presumably by sea-action;
it now weighs 225g
Girona

6.14 POWDER-SCOOP, Copper
455mm l
An oval sheet of copper bent along
its long axis to form a more than
semicircular-sectioned scoop;
abraded and pitted at the leading
edge
La Trinidad Valencera

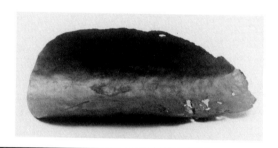

6.15 LINSTOCK, Wood
90mm l
The front end of a linstock for
applying a lighted slow-match to the
touch-hole of a gun, in the form of
the head of a grotesque animal; a
length of match survives in the
gaping jaw of the animal, like a
small tongue
La Trinidad Valencera

6.16 LINSTOCK, Wood
450mm l
The greater part of a linstock,
though the final part of the handle is
missing, in the form of a clenched
fist with an aperture within its grasp
to hold the slow-match
La Trinidad Valencera

6.17 SHOT-GAUGE, Wood
120mm d (interior)
Circle of wood 10mm thick, with a
forked handle at the top on which is
inscribed the Roman numeral 'XV';
for measuring the size of shot for a
specific gun and to ensure its
regularity
La Trinidad Valencera

6.18 SHOT-GAUGE, Wood
92mm d (interior)
As above but 12mm thick and with
a perforation but no numeral on the
handle
La Trinidad Valencera

6.19 SHOT-GAUGE, Wood
46mm d (interior)
As above but 8mm thick; no marks
La Trinidad Valencera

6.20 GUNNER'S RULE, Wood
90mm l (the largest portion)
Three fragments of a gunner's rule,
with calibrations ranging from 50 to
120 clearly visible
La Trinidad Valencera

6.21 SHOT, Iron
40mm d; 230g
Round of spherical cast iron shot;
for the Esmeril
Girona

6.22 SHOT, Iron
70mm d; 1200g
As above but not for one of the guns
recovered
Girona

6.23 SHOT, Iron
95mm d; 2,250g
As above but not for one of the guns
recovered
Girona

6.24 SHOT, Iron
130mm d; 7,450g
As above but not for one of the guns
recovered
Girona

6.25 SHOT, Iron
63mm d; 750g
As above but not for one of the guns
recovered
La Trinidad Valencera

6.26 SHOT, Iron
75mm d; 1350g
As above; for the Swivel Gun
La Trinidad Valencera

6.27 SHOT, Iron
95mm d; 3550g
As above but not for one of the guns
recovered
La Trinidad Valencera

6.28 SHOT, Iron
155mm d; 10450g
As above but not for one of the guns
recovered
La Trinidad Valencera

6.29 SHOT, Iron
172mm d; 2750g x 2
Cast iron shot cut in two, with
section polished to show cooling
rings in cast iron
Santa Maria de la Rosa

6.30 SHOT, Stone
95mm d; 450g
Spherical stone shot
Girona

6.31 SHOT, Stone
116mm d; 2400g
As above
Girona

6.32 SHOT, Stone
85mm d; 1000g
As above
La Trinidad Valencera

6.33 SHOT, Stone
155mm d; 5400g
As above
La Trinidad Valencera

**6.34 CANISTER SHOT, Wood
and Iron**
250mm l
Hexagonal box of wood, about
90mm in diameter, filled with iron
shrapnel, now solidified into a solid
mass
La Trinidad Valencera

**6.35 TOUCH-HOLE PRICKER,
Copper**
185mm l
Skewer-like copper rod with circular
handle for cleaning out touch-holes
of ordnance
La Trinidad Valencera

6.36 SPONGE-HEAD, Wood
420mm l
Cylindrical block of wood, rounded
at the end, 90mm in diameter, for
cleaning barrels of guns
La Trinidad Valencera

6.37 SPONGE-HEAD, Wood
450mm l
As above
La Trinidad Valencera

6.38 GUN-CARRIAGE WHEEL,
Wood and Iron
1093mm d
Large composite wooden wheel,
120mm t, fitted with an iron tyre
110mm w; wheel has 10 spokes,
each morticed in place, meeting at a
central hub, 240mm d at
extremities, 110mm d, with
provision for an axle 80mm in
diameter
La Trinidad Valencera

6.39 GUN-CARRIAGE WHEEL,
Wood and Iron
1360mm d
Similar to above but larger
La Trinidad Valencera

6.40 GOATSKIN, Animal Tissue
360mm w
Two pieces of goatskin covered with
long black hair; used for cleaning
the guns
La Trinidad Valencera

CHAPTER 7
Small Arms and Invasion Equipment

That the Armada was basically an invasion fleet, whose objective was to land in and occupy England, must never be forgotten. Of the 130 ships listed as composing this mighty fleet, all but the smallest zabras and pinazas carried soldiers as well as sailors. These vessels, including the two pinazas in the Squadron of Guipuzcoa, the *Nuestra Senora de Guadalupe* and the *Magdalena*, as well as the eight or so smallest zabras in the Squadron of Pataches and Zabras, had crews of fewer than 25 (with one exception, *La Concepcion de Somanila*, which had 31). They also carried only one or two guns, or none at all. Their functions were such that they required soldiers neither for offence nor defence.

All the other ships did carry soldiers, to a total of 19,295. For the most part the soldiers were embarked in contingents of between one hundred and three hundred, with many of the smaller ships carrying less than a hundred. Some of the larger ships carried over 300; two ships, not by any means the largest in the fleet, the *San Felipe* (800 tons) and the *Florencia* (961 tons), carried 415 and 400 respectively. The whole force was organised into 5 tercios of heavy infantry, encompassing the pikemen, arquebusiers and musketeers. Each tercio, of roughly 3,000 men, was commanded by a *maestre de campo*. The balance of this sea-borne army consisted of light infantry and support groups – pioneers and the like. The whole force was under the command of Don Francisco de Bobadilla, the *Maestre de Campo General*, a man described by the Duke of Medina Sidonia as 'a man of considerable experience, both at sea and on land'. He is also the man who is thought to have been responsible for the ruthless practice of leaving crippled Armada ships to fend for themselves.

The intention was that an army of 30,000 from Flanders would be added to the force carried from Lisbon in the Armada. Commanded by the governor of the Spanish Netherlands, Alexander Farnese, Duke of Parma and Piacenza, this was to be assembled at Dunkirk and embarked at Nieuport, to cross the Channel in a flotilla of invasion barges under the protection of the fleet. This army of Parma's in the Netherlands was the most formidable in Europe, consisting of totally professional, battle-tempered warriors of many different nationalities – German, Walloon, Spanish, Italian and Irish. Even 30,000 of these would constitute a grave threat to England if landed there together with further 20,000 men from Spain itself.

An army of this size, 50,000 in all, would require a considerable amount of equipment and supplies. While the main bulk of these supplies was to be carried by the Squadron of Urcas, much was also spread among the other vessels, especially the large freighters pressed into service with the Armada, such as the Venetian merchantmen *La Trinidad Valencera* and *La Lavia*. In all it is reckoned that some 7,000 muskets and arquebuses were packed into ships' holds, together with the lead, powder and match required; a total of 1,232 quintals (roughly a hundredweight) of lead (each galleass alone was allotted 15 quintals, although Robert Stenuit states that when she left Naples the *Girona* was carrying 30 '*quintaux de plomb pour fondre les balles en Augleterre*'), 5,600 quintals of fine-grained powder, for priming both small arms and heavy ordnances, and 1,200 of match, as well as some 10,000 pikes and muskets. In addition there were field and siege guns and their limbers, with mules to help draw them and the wagons. Tents, spades, axes and other tools and equipment necessary for siege-works were also part of the burden.

An example of the kind of equipment carried is contained in the manifests of several of the ships, preserved in the Archives in Simancas. That for *La Trinidad Valencera* is particularly of interest, since so many of the items listed have survived and been preserved.

The entries are in rather haphazard order, as a reflection of the order in which they were loaded, more or less as supplies became available, or as a reflection of their being stowed in different places in the ship. Some of the entries relating to small arms are as follows:

8 quintals of arquebus powder
4 quintals of arquebus match
20 cutlasses
21 arrovas 4lb of arquebus shot in wooden barrels
10 arrovas 80lb of musket shot in wooden barrels
100 new arquebuses with their cleaning gear, flasks and small flasks and shot moulds
20 muskets with their cleaning gear, flasks and small flasks, shot moulds and forked supports
400 new ash pikes with their iron heads and butts
116 1lb of arquebus match
165 quintals of arquebus powder

The physical remains of the small arms include, from the *Girona*, a well-preserved arquebus stock, complete with ramrod (Cat 7.1). On this site its survival is little short of miraculous; its initial recovery was a small triumph of patience and dedication on the part of Robert Stenuit:

> One day, at the far end of the site, on Lacada Point, sticking out from under a protective coating of black magma, harder than stone, made of rusted cannon balls, kitchen debris (animal bones, charcoal, broken pots) and cartridges, and cemented again by the gunpowder, I spotted a small piece of wood. 'Part of an oar,' I motioned to Maurice. He came and looked. 'No,' he waved, putting an imaginary gun to his shoulder. The next day, after three hours work with a hammer and a chisel I had uncovered six inches of an arquebus stock. On the third day, having worked my fingers sore to get through that dense mass, I could see the chamber. All that was left of the barrel was a grey paste sticking to the wood and to the rock. It was disintegrating before my very eyes with every movement of the swell. The firing piece had gone down loaded. I found the round lead ball still in the breech. Working at the rate I was, it took me the rest of the week to finish digging it out. Then, firing piece in hand, I swam up and in pantomime fired a victory salvo into the air.

The arquebus was duly conserved in the laboratory, complete with its ramrod and the round of lead shot that had been in the chamber. The wooden stock is complete, 1,135mm long, and the ramrod 847mm long; the lead ball is 16mm calibre. While the 'grey paste' that constituted the steel barrel and firing mechanism has disappeared for ever, the holes and slots to receive it are still in the wood, as though ready to receive a new barrel and firing mechanism, thanks to skilled conservation techniques.

Of the two types of firearm used in the sixteenth century, the arquebus was the lighter and more elegant; the musket – though the word is often used, inaccurately, as a general term, rather as 'cannon' is used indiscrimately for ordnance – was a much heavier type, both in terms of size of ball fired and of the actual weight of the weapon. It was so much heavier, in fact, that while the arquebus could be fired from the shoulder and held in the hand like a modern rifle, the musket, in the strict sense, required a stand to support its weight. 'A terrible arm and heavy to the one who carried it,' a sixteenth-century Spaniard once wrote. The musket fired a ball roughly four times the weight of the arquebus, approximately 60g as opposed to 15g. However, both weapons were muzzle-loaders and, in general, the firing mechanism was what is known as a 'matchlock'; a burning slow-match of braided hemp impregnated with salt-petre, held in the jaws of a curved metal arm or 'serpentine', was brought into contact with a small priming charge in the pan, by pulling a lever or trigger. While the matchlock may have been a rather cumbersome, if not dangerous, method of firing a gun, requiring rigorous training, it was relatively cheap to produce and remained in service with armies throughout Europe long after more sophisticated devices had been perfected (the 'lowest tender syndrome' at work again). Small wonder that the Duke of Medina Sidonia had enjoined that officers ensured that 'the soldiers' arms are kept clean, ready for service; and cleaned twice a week in any case', and 'must also exercise their men in the use of their arms, so that they may be expert when needed'.

A similar arquebus was found on the site of the *Santa Maria de la Rosa*; it too had been loaded, but unfortunately it has not survived. However, from *La Trinidad Valencera* came several arquebus and musket stocks, though for the most part only the butt end, being the thickest portion, has survived (Cat 7.2–7.4). These are likely to have been part of the cargo of invasion equipment on *La Trinidad Valencera*, examples of the twenty muskets, with their supports, and the hundred new arquebuses loaded onto the ship, complete with cleaning gear and iron bullet-moulds. The arquebuses from the *Girona* and the *Santa Maria de la Rosa*, on the other hand, must have been already in service; both were fully loaded and there were several incidents during the fighting in the Channel when they may have been employed.

That small arms fire was exchanged is demonstrated eloquently by some of the lead shot yielded by several of the Armada wrecks so far explored, *El Gran Grifon* in Shetland, as well as the Irish wrecks of the *Santa Maria de la Rosa* and the *Girona*. Among the many rounds of lead shot recovered are examples that have been totally flattened by impact (Cat 7.13). This suggests that, during one or other of the actions which were almost hand-to-hand, these Spanish ships had been the recipients of volley after volley from English muskets and arquebuses; the shot, after impact, had lodged in the ships' timbers until, in the course of time, they separated or rotted; the impacted shot then fell heavily to the next surface beneath. Not all the lead shot, of course, is impacted; among that recovered from the various wrecks there is perfectly preserved shot of a variety of calibres (Cat 7.7–7.10), 12mm, 14mm and 20mm for the most part, while from the *Girona* came a scatter of very small shot, a little larger than modern shotgun pellets (Cat 7.11). Also from the *Girona* came a good indication that shot was actually cast on board – three rounds of shot in the 'as cast' condition, still joined together by the trails of lead which solidified in the little channel feeding each matrix of the mould (Cat 7.12). Unfortunately from none of the Armada wrecks has there appeared a shot-mould such as was recovered from the *Mary Rose*. Many of the rounds retain their casting flashes, where the two opposing faces of the mould had not been in perfect register; many also retain a small stalk where the trail of lead was broken off.

Among the supplies of lead carried on the *Girona*, in addition to the hundredweight ingots (presumably the equivalent of a single quintal), there were roughly rectangular plates of lead, about half a metre long and weighing about 8kg (Cat 4.34). Blocks of this size and weight would have been feasible for arquebusiers and musketeers to carry in addition to their other burdens, though it is possible that these flat plates may have constituted part of the protection of the ship's hull, as a sort of combined fixed ballast and protective layer. They do, however, seem to conform to the description of 'planchas' – plates or slabs of lead often encountered. (The *Girona*, despite the considerable quantity of lead recovered, appears not to have carried any of the large rectangular blocks of nearly 3 quintals weight described as appearing among the material from the *Santa Maria de la Rosa*.)

Some of the smaller shot recovered may have been for pistol, for while no pistol as such has been found, two leather pouches or holsters were recovered from *La Trinidad Valencera* (Cat 7.19–7.20). Each is of thick leather, stitched together to form an open-ended trapezoidal tube; both had plaited cords attached. The matchlock would, of course, have been singularly inappropriate for pistols; the notion of a man parading the deck, for instance, with a burning slow-match at his waist would have been, at least, impracticable. It is likely that any pistols would have been wheellocks. In these the spark needed to ignite the priming powder next to the touch-hole was supplied by the rotation of a serrated, eponymous wheel against a piece of iron pyrites. Once the mechanism had been wound up, or 'spanned', by a key, the pistol could be carried and fired off at will simply by squeezing the trigger. While wheellocks are the most likely type of firing mechanism for pistols aboard Armada ships, it is just possible that either the snaphance or the flintlock itself, of which the snaphance was an early form, could have been in use; both were known and both appear in portraits of the period. Despite the presence of the two holsters among the material from *La Trinidad Valencera*, and the suggestion that they indicate the existence of pistols, there is a reference in the 1587 *Instrucion Nautica* of Diego Garcia de Palacio, to pistols not being common on board ship at that time. When he is discussing 'the ship that attacks', he remarks that the captain 'will arm the squads with breast-plates, morions, swords, daggers, targets and pistols (if he has them)' and, as J. Bankston, the translator and editor, says, 'this has to be one of the earliest mentions of pistols being used in maritime warfare'.

The other accoutrement for firearms recovered from *La Trinidad Valencera* was a series of powder flasks, of different sizes and capacities. These are made of thin sheets of wood, about 2.5mm thick, nailed together to form a hollow container, more or less triangular in shape; the front and back plates are fastened to the sides by little metal pins (Cat 7.17–7.18). They may, originally, have been covered with leather to make them leakproof and to help keep the powder dry. The metal device which would have been fitted to the top for pouring and measuring the powder and to close the flask has not survived. Such powder flasks can be seen hanging from the belts of musketeers in sixteenth-century illustrations; indeed the poor musketeer must have been dreadfully burdened with the items necessary for his trade. While the preserved flasks are of different sizes, these sizes do not seem sufficiently different for them to be distinguished as the 'flasks and small flasks' detailed in *La Trinidad Valencera*'s inventory.

'To make fine gunpowder for handgunnes', 'more finer gunpowder for hand-gunnes' and 'fine corne powder for handgunnes of that sort of grosse gunpow-der' are three special treatments described by Lucar in his treatise on gunnery published in 1588. All entail 'beating' the powder and in one recipe Lucar specifies that the beating should be done in a 'morter of brasse'. Two small bronze mortars recovered from the *Girona* may well be exactly the sort he had in mind (Cat 7.15–7.16); the accompanying bronze pestle (Cat 7.14) may well have been used to do the beating. The insistence on using brass or bronze mortars is a perfectly understandable safety measure, to eliminate the risk of the sparks that might be struck from an iron or steel mortar.

What makes this material particularly interesting – and this is true of so many artefacts from excavated sites, whether on land or under the sea – is that it is, for the most part, standard issue, the kind of mass-produced equipment common to all armies. Most of the early firearms, and indeed other arms, that have been preserved in museums and private collections are the ornate and decorated types, prized more for their artistic adornment than for anything else. They give a totally erroneous impression of the grim seriousness of killing at the lowest cost that has always been the objective of armies.

'Edged weapons' are also represented among the Armada material, though in every case the edges themselves have not survived. From the *Girona* came a series of dagger-hilts of several designs, but basically the same sort of construc-tion (Cat 7.26–7.28). Each hilt consists of a wooden core, in which is preserved the only remanent portion of the steel blade, part of the tang still in place. This wooden core is carefully covered with metallic wire in a number of different ways. In one the wooden core is carefully wrapped with a double-stranded copper wire, spirally twisted; at each end the same spirally twisted wire has been made into a plait consisting of three strands, each of three lengths of the wire; this hilt was found with its sheath, tapering sleeve of fine leather sewn together over a core of thin wood. One of the other hilts is similar to the first, but the wooden core is wrapped with silver wire and slightly more of the dagger's steel survives. The third is altogether a more complex creation, even though the wire is only of copper. The covering was made by wrapping round the wooden core a series of bands, each consisting of eight fine wires; through these, over and under, like basketwork, were woven four strands of double, spirally twisted, copper wire, laid side-by-side.

Also from the *Girona* were recovered fragments of silver sword-guards – curved fragments of cast silver, one of which terminates in the head of a serpent or monster (Cat 7.23–7.24). These were obviously parts either of the knuckle-guards or of the quillons of sword-guards, of a type well-known, not merely from portraits, but from preserved examples in museums and private collections. Since they are of silver, these presumably came from a better class of sword, belonging to an officer. *La Trinidad Valencera*, to enhance the complementary nature of the material from the two wrecks, produced two sword-hangers (Cat 7.21–7.22). These are both of fine leather and are preserved so that what is missing from one can be inferred from the other. The more complete example is almost like a glove with four fingers; the outer surface is decorated with stamped star-motifs of different sizes, while the 'fingers' bear impressed simple lyre patterns. The other is similar, but less well preserved. However, unlike the first, it does retain a portion of the fine leather strap, to which still adheres a piece of metal which may be the remains of a hook by which it was fastened to the sword-belt.

Of the 400 new pikes of ash, needless to say, neither heads nor ferrules (butts) of iron have survived. A number of portions of wooden poles may represent all that has survived of this consignment. A picture of the Spanish troops marching in precise formation, after the landing at Terceira in 1583, shows clearly how the pikemen might have been deployed in the advance on London. With musketeers and arquebusiers in columns around a solid square of pikemen, the Spanish sent the Portuguese scurrying into the hills. There is a reference in the manifest of *La Trinidad Valencera* to '*dos fexes de arcos de castano*', bows of chestnut, which bring to mind the boxes of longbows discovered on the English warship the *Mary Rose*. So far, however, no actual examples of bows have been recovered from the site of *La Trinidad Valencera* or of any of the other excavated Armada wrecks. Cross-bows, examples of which have been recovered from the 1554 Texas wrecks, have not been identified as yet among the material from the Irish wrecks.

Among the more exotic small arms carried were two kinds of incendiary devices (Cat 7.32–7.33). The first is a small ceramic pot, globular, but waisted, presumably to make it easier to hold firmly (dropping any grenade can have unfortunate consequences); this was filled with highly combustible materials, for which the estimable Lucar gives a recipe, with an assortment of fuses, or 'gunmatches of a finger in length', to ignite the contents. The use of such weapons on wooden sixteenth-century ships, and the smaller ones were prescribed specifically for use at sea, with highly combustible materials on every side – sails, rigging, not to mention magazines full of gunpowder – must have been nearly as hazardous for the giver as to the receiver. Another, rather globular, handled pot of earthenware, also from *La Trinidad Valencera* (Cat 7.34), may also have been a fire-pot. The other incendiary device, known as a 'bomba', was similar to a firework on a pole. A wooden cylinder, about 0.75m long and about 10cm in diameter, was filled with highly combustible materials and the fuse lit. Then the device, mounted on the end of a pole, was thrust at the enemy, spitting fire and flame; the pole withdrawn, the enemy was left to extinguish it if he could or die in the attempt. These are probably the two incendiary devices referred to in the Trinidad's manifest:

25 incendiary alcanzias
5 incendiary bombas
4 measures of hemp
5 spare tubes for the bombas

Fire-raising was obviously not a peculiarly English technique.

Materials and equipment for the invasion are sometimes difficult to separate from that which might also be used on board, although consignments of 20 trimming axes or 100 timber stakes for awnings suggest that they may have been intended as invasion supplies. Some items are quite explicitly described as being intended for use on the part of the campaign to take place on land:

2 campaign tents with their skirts and poles
6 timber gun-carriages for the campaign
6 timber limbers [?] for the campaign
1 siege-engine with axles and wheels

Palpable gun-carriages and assorted wheels have been observed on the sites both of *La Trinidad Valencera* and of the *Juliana* at Streedagh and portions of the gun-carriages, including axles and wheels, have been raised from *La Trinidad Valencera*, but are still undergoing conservation. Whether some of the wheels from this site may have belonged to limbers (if that is the correct translation of '*seis lonjas de madera gaurnezidas de fierro par servicio de los armones*') is unknown. Some of those observed might even belong to the rather enigmatic siege-engine.

One puzzling find from *La Trinidad Valencera* was a shapeless, matted lump of textile, which, because of the fact that it was equipped with little wooden toggles, cords and small leather patches, was known as 'the duffel coat' (Cat 7.29). Closer examination, and subsequent treatment, at the Textile Conservation Centre suggested a different, more fascinating, interpretation.

When this object was found on the sea-bed in 1978, its successful extraction required very careful work. First it was undercut, by excavating sand away from underneath it, then a metal plate was slipped underneath and a covering of muslin pegged over the top to secure it during the lift. It was kept wet all the time on its way from Kinnagoe to Belfast and from Belfast to Hampton Court. There its initial examination provoked this description:

In appearance this object is a brown amorphous mass consisting of fabric and mud compressed together with short sections of rope, small wooden toggles and small squares of leather embedded in it. It measures approximately 71 x 43 x 5cm at its greatest dimensions and consists of several chunks varying in size. There is one major section with three smaller pieces, which though detached still lie in place.

As the investigation continued it transpired that the plain woven fabric of which it was mainly composed was probably of hemp or jute which appeared to have been treated with a copper solution. The rope was of two kinds, one heavier than the other, and was probably of nettle-fibre. All in all, it appeared that it was likely to be a tent: copper solutions are known to have been used to waterproof tents; the ropes suggest guy-ropes, with some heavier than the others; and the small leather patches, some square with one perforation, some rectangular with two, and associated with lengths of rope, were obviously reinforcements, as is found with modern tents to prevent tearing at points of strain. It proved impossible to assess the original size of the suggested tent, but it has been likened to a Turkish tent of 1598 which has many similar structural details. The temptation to identify it as one of the two campaign tents in the manifest is overpowering. There is, moreover, from the site, an abundance of wooden objects closely resembling tent-pegs. As a tent it is more likely to have been used for storing munitions than sheltering people.

Much of the other equipment carried on *La Trinidad Valencera* and the other ships would, of course, have been highly useful for the invading army; the siege guns cast by Remigy de Halut, after all, were made specifically for this purpose. Much of the powder, shot and match must have been held in reserve for the landings and subsequent projected march on London, which is, perhaps, why so much is still to be found on the various wreck-sites.

The size and scope of this invasion force and its meticulously inventoried equipment would naturally seem a threat of the gravest moment to the English. Against this massive force of battle-seasoned veterans, armed with the best equipment and arms that gold and silver from the New World could buy, were ranged, for the most part, hastily erected defences and the 'trained bands', armed, in some instances, with home-forged pikes and pitch-forks. But how much more serious a threat it must have seemed, even after its rather fruitless and inglorious departure from the English Channel, to scantily defended Ireland, with a native population only too eager to receive support from a powerful foreign ally.

Sources used for Chapter 7

Arnold, J.B., and Weddle, R.S., *The Nautical Archaeology of Padre Island*, London, 1978

Bankston, J., *Nautical Instruction 1587*, Arizona, 1986

Flanagan, L., Martin, C. and Stenuit, R., *Les Tresors de l'Armada*, Brussels, 1985

Mann, Sir J., *Wallace Collection Catalogues: European Arms and Armour,*
    London, 1962
Martin, C., *Full Fathom Five,* London, 1975
Stenuit, R., *Treasures of the Armada,* London, 1974
Walker, B., *The Armada,* Amsterdam, 1982

Small Arms and Invasion Equipment

7.1 ARQUEBUS-STOCK, Wood
1135mm l
Complete wooden stock of an
arquebus (the lighter of the two
forms of hand-gun); with it is its
ramrod, 847mm l, and the lead ball
found in the chamber, 16mm
calibre. While none of the metal
parts, the barrel and the firing-
mechanism, have survived, the
housings for them are well
preserved. The barrel end is
straight, with a slight curve to the
butt
Girona

7.2 ARQUEBUS-STOCK, Wood
526mm+ l
The butt-end of an arquebus-stock;
again the metallic parts have not
survived but their housings are clear
La Trinidad Valencera

7.3 ARQUEBUS-STOCK, Wood
365mm+ l
As above, but with slightly heavier
and more sharply curved butt
La Trinidad Valencera

7.4 MUSKET-STOCK, Wood
330mm+ l
Apparently the butt-end of the stock
of the heavier type of handgun,
which required a forked support for
firing; the butt is much heavier than
those above and more sharply
defined
La Trinidad Valencera

7.5 ARQUEBUS-BARREL, Steel
89mm+ l
Portion of the barrel of an arquebus
of 10mm calibre
La Trinidad Valencera

7.6 RAMROD, Wood
486mm+ l
Ramrod of a musket or arquebus,
originally straight, now slightly
curved; one end is broken, the other
is pointed
La Trinidad Valencera

7.7 ARQUEBUS SHOT, Lead
14mm d; 13.56g (average)
Eight of several thousand such shot
recovered; on one the casting-flash is
clearly visible
Girona

7.8 ARQUEBUS SHOT, Lead
12mm d; 13.08g (average)
Two of numerous shot recovered of
small calibre
La Trinidad Valencera

7.9 ARQUEBUS SHOT, Lead
15mm d; 18.05g (average)
Three of numerous medium calibre
shot recovered
La Trinidad Valencera

7.10 MUSKET SHOT, Lead
20mm d; 47.26g
Shot of large calibre; the casting-
flash is visible
La Trinidad Valencera

7.11 PELLETS, Lead
5mm d; 18.68g (total)
19 pellets of roughly 5mm d,
resembling modern shot-gun pellets,
presumably used as scatter shot
Girona

7.12 ARQUEBUS SHOT, Lead
14mm d; 69g (total)
Three rounds of arquebus shot as
cast, still joined by the runner of
lead from the mould
Girona

7.13 MUSKET SHOT, Lead
11.32g
Nine examples out of many of
impacted lead shot, presumably
discharged from English guns at the
Girona during skirmishes in the
Channel; it lodged in the planking,
having flattened on impact, and
then, as the ship's structure
collapsed, fell to the bottom
Girona

7.14 PESTLE, Bronze
109mm l
Bronze pestle of simple elongated
pear-shape
Girona

7.15 MORTAR, Bronze
101mm d
A simple flat-bottomed circular disk
of bronze with a shallow concave
top, probably for grinding powder,
with a bronze pestle, to avoid the
risk of sparks
Girona

7.16 MORTAR, Bronze
80mm d
As above but lighter and better
preserved
Girona

7.17 POWDER-FLASK, Wood
104mm h
Composite powder flask, made of
thin plates of wood about 2.5mm
thick; the front and back plates are
more or less triangular, with curved
sides and fastened to the side and
base plates with metal nails; remains
of other little nails or tacks suggest
that it may originally have been
covered with leather. The metal
measuring device for the top has not
survived
La Trinidad Valencera

7.18 POWDER-FLASK, Wood
178mm h
As above but larger and stouter; the
wooden plates are about 5mm thick;
while the metal fittings have not
survived, the top has and carries an
opening of 18mm d
La Trinidad Valencera

7.19 HOLSTER (?), Leather
185mm l
A sort of trapezoidal tube, open at
top and bottom, made of two pieces
of thick leather sewn together; has
been repaired with a piece of thick
leather; a piece of plaited cord was
found with it
La Trinidad Valencera

7.20 HOLSTER (?), Leather
225mm l
As above, also containing a length of
plaited cord no longer attached
La Trinidad Valencera

7.21 SWORD-HANGER, Leather
22mm l
Rectangular piece of fairly fine
leather, more or less glove-shaped,
with four 'fingers'; the main part is
covered with stamped star-motifs of
two different sizes, while the
pendant fingers bear stars and a
simple lyre-pattern
La Trinidad Valencera

7.22 SWORD-HANGER, Leather
530mm l (strap)
As above but less well preserved;
does, however, retain a leather strap
some 19mm wide; a piece of almost
totally mineralised steel adheres to
the leather
La Trinidad Valencera

7.23 SWORD-GUARD, Silver
111mm l; 38.22g
Portion of a silver sword-guard, the
main part of double-curved silver
rod terminating in three knops or
bosses, through the centre of the
middle of which a thin silver rivet
passes. The other end is straight,
coming from the curved section at a
sharp angle and terminating in a
bestial head; a loose silver ring rides
over the body
Girona

7.24 SWORD-GUARD, Silver
57mm l; 14.42g
The central section of a knuckle-
guard of a sword, consisting of a
length of round-sectioned silver bar
of ogee shape, with a central knop
on either side of which is a leaf-
pattern
Girona

7.25 DAGGER-SHEATH, Leather
262mm l
A tapering sleeve of fine leather,
stitched at the back over a core of
two pieces of wood. Found with the
following object
Girona

7.26 DAGGER-HILT, Copper, Steel and Wood

84mm l

Consists of a central tapering core, which retains a portion of the steel tang of the dagger; this core has been covered with a double, spirally twisted, copper wire; at each end there is a plait of three elements of this double wire

Girona

7.27 DAGGER-HILT, Silver, Steel and Wood

86mm l

As above but retains not only the remains of the tang of the dagger but a portion of the guard as well; the treatment of the core is similar except that the wire is of silver

Girona

7.28 DAGGER-HILT, Copper and Wood

79mm l

As above, but there are no traces of the dagger; the core is covered with woven copper wire: bands of eight fine wires circle the core, through these are woven bands consisting of four rows of twisted double wire. The end of the hilt is finished with a three-element plait of double twisted wire

Girona

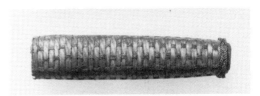

7.29 TENT, Hemp, Nettle-fibre, Leather and Wood

710mm w

An amorphous mass of fibre in which, in the course of conservation, certain features were recognised: the major part of the mass is of fabric, of jute or hemp, of a plain weave of z-twist; traces of copper were

discovered in the fabric suggesting a
proofing-treatment. To the fabric in
places were stitched reinforcing
squares or rectangles of leather;
through holes in these two sizes of
rope, evidently of nettle-fibre, were
found, a light one and one three
times as heavy, suggesting main
guys and lighter guys. Attached to
some portions of rope were small
wooden toggles. It has not been
possible to estimate the erected size
of the tent. *La Trinidad* was carrying
'*dos tientas de campagna*' (two
campaign tents); it is likely this was
one
La Trinidad Valencera

7.30 TOGGLE, Wood
38mm l
A small cylindrical piece of wood
with a central groove, tapering
towards each end, which terminate
in a slight mushroom
La Trinidad Valencera

7.31 TENT-PEGS, Wood
310–360mm l
Four of a number of crudely made
pegs, presumably for the tent; each
has been roughly sharpened at one
end
La Trinidad Valencera

7.32 FIRE-POT OR HAND-GRENADE, Pottery
111mm h
Small sharply waisted pot of glazed
earthenware, with a short neck and
everted rim; the pot has been rather
carelessly thrown and equally
carelessly covered (partially) inside
and out with a brown glaze. The pot
would have been filled with highly
inflammable materials, fitted with

lengths of slow match as fuses and
thrown onto enemy ships
La Trinidad Valencera

7.33 INCENDIARY TUBE, Wood
740mm l
A cylindrical tube of wood, 800mm
wide at the mouth, with a narrower
'handle', 165mm l. The tube was
bound tightly at 4 places on the
thick end and at one on the handle.
In action the tube would be
mounted on a pole, filled with
explosives, the fuse lit and the whole
thing thrust at the enemy ship, the
carrying pole withdrawn
La Trinidad Valencera

7.34 FIRE-POT OR GRENADE,
Pottery
140mm d
Squat globular earthenware
container, apparently unglazed; at
one side is a small handle with an
uncomfortably small opening. The
base is slightly convex. The neck
and shoulder of the pot bear quite
sharply incised lines, the body is
lightly grooved
La Trinidad Valencera

7.35 MUSKET, Wood, Steel and
Concretion
862mm l
A large musket-shaped piece of
concretion in which, as shown by
X-radiography, is contained a
musket complete with its firing-
mechanism. The polished section cut
from the end shows an octagonal (on
the outside) steel barrel in place in a
wooden stock, also octagonal; the
ramrod is still in place in its holder
La Trinidad Valencera

CHAPTER 8
Victualling and Provisions

For a campaign scheduled to last for six months, involving some 30,000 men, the task of victualling and equipping the 130 ships of the Armada was clearly a gargantuan task.It had been begun by Alvaro de Bazan, Marquis of Santa Cruz, the man who had conceived the idea which was to become the Spanish Armada of 1588. His original plan was costed at 3,800,000 ducats, for a force consisting of 94,222 men, more than three times the number who were to participate in the actuality. The provision list for this provisional plan was formidable: biscuit, 373,337 cwt; bacon, 22,800 cwt; cheese, 21,500 cwt; tuna, 23,200 barrels; salt beef, 16,040 cwt; beans, peas and rice, 66,000 bushels; water 2,200,000 gallons; and wine 5,148,000 gallons.

Supplies, not only of food, but also containers and mess-equipment with which to consume it had to be organised. This was in addition to assembling the necessary ordnance, the powder, the shot, the match; the equipment for the invading army, the transport, the small arms. It was clearly an administrative exercise of the greatest complexity and one that required time, money and freedom from additional outside difficulties. Neither Santa Cruz, who died in office, nor his successor, the Duke of Medina Sidonia, had much of any of these.

In the first place, despite the enormous wealth flowing in from the Americas, even Spain was chronically short of money; the maintenance of a very sizeable army in the Netherlands was a constant drain and the promised subvention from the Pope, Sextus V, never materialised. In the second place, Philip's allocation of time for the preparations was totally unrealistic. In the third place there was Drake.

It would never have been easy to conceal the fact that an enormous fleet was being assembled at Lisbon. All of Europe knew what was going on: the English knew; even the Irish knew, for there are many references to Irish seamen reporting on the activities in Spain.

Inevitably the temptation to interfere as much as possible with the Spanish plans, and if possible thereby make a profit, was irresistible to both Drake and Elizabeth; Drake had, after all, carried out a similar, successful and profitable piece of 'interference' before, in 1585 when he had relieved the Spanish of some of their gold. The plot was hatched between them. In April 1587, Drake went to sea with a force of 23 ships and 2,200 men 'to impeach the purpose of the Spanish fleet and stop their meeting at Lisbon'. Among his squadron, which was, after all, nearly one-fifth the size of the Armada, were four well-armed royal warships – the *Elizabeth Bonaventure*, the *Golden Lion*, the *Dreadnought* and the *Revenge*, all between 400 and 500 English tons – as well as armed merchantmen. This formidable little force set off for the Iberian peninsula and by 26 April was reconnoitring off Lisbon, where the Armada was assembling. Lisbon, of course, was too well guarded to be easy meat; the Torre de Belem, guarding the mouth of the Tagus was well armed. The fleet continued, therefore, to Cadiz, in the extreme south of Spain.

By this time, of course, Drake was well out of reach of the countermanding orders issued by Elizabeth forbidding him to enter a Spanish harbour or land on Spanish soil. Quite fortuitously, these had reached Plymouth after he had set sail.

The harbour of Cadiz was crammed with shipping, some with only skeleton crews, some without guns fitted, others with no sails. The English squadron sailed in, guns blazing, and sank or set on fire the Spanish ships in the outer harbour. Those worth it were looted and six supply ships full of provisions were captured. In the inner harbour, the flagship of Santa Cruz was being fitted out and this was set on fire. It seemed a remarkable, and a remarkably easy, victory – until the wind dropped completely as they were preparing to leave. The Spanish galleys, so despised by Drake for real war at sea, crept out to harass the English squadron and fire-ships were sent into its midst. It looked as if victory was to slip from their grasp. However, fortunately for them, a breeze came up and they were able to slip out, with their prizes. While claims and counter-claims of the damage done were made, even the Spanish admitted that 24 ships were destroyed, to a value of 172,000 ducats.

Much of the shipping and supplies for the Armada were converging on Lisbon, the assembly point, from ports in the Mediterranean; Venice, Naples and Milan in Italy, ports on the eastern coast of Spain itself like Barcelona and Cartagena, as well as those in places like Sicily. To reach Lisbon it all had to come through the Strait of Gibraltar. Drake resolved to lie in wait and inflict as much damage as possible on this strategic traffic. To this end he needed a secure land-base, where he could, at least, take on fresh water. His first choice, Lagos, proved to be too heavily defended, so he settled on Sagres, right on the tip of Cape St Vincent. Here a castle and library had been built by the Portuguese prince known as Henry the Navigator, the unsanctified saint of seafarers. The library no longer existed, but the castle still commanded the small bay Drake wanted to use as an anchorage. He succeeded in taking the castle, by the kind of unorthodox means of which he was a master.

For three weeks Drake was master of the seas between the Strait and Lisbon and his blockade was successful. Apart from the smaller shipping, much of the traffic refused to pass Cadiz; of those smaller vessels, the English destroyed more than a hundred. The worst damage they inflicted to the Spanish war-effort, however, was the destruction of 1,700 tons of barrel staves and hoops, and of the Portuguese tuna fisheries, devastating both the nets and the boats that tended them. These were severe blows: the wood for casks had to be well seasoned to be effective in preserving the provisions stored in them, especially water; tuna was to be one of the main sources of protein for the Spanish fleet.

The blockade, however, was both too boring and too unprofitable for the English squadron. Drake decided to go for more attractive booty. He headed for the Azores in quest of treasure galleons. He found one, the *San Felipe*, a very large Portuguese carrack, possibly of as much as 1,400 tons, laden with pepper, cinnamon, silk, ivory, calico and with a reasonable fortune in gold, silver and precious stones. So laden was she, indeed, that her gun-ports could not be used. After a token resistance, her captain surrendered and the prize was seized. The total value, back in London, was some £114,000. This would have been enough, at the time, to build nine ships the size of Drake's flagship.

Drake's little adventure, therefore, had cost the Spanish not only ships and money, of both of which they were dreadfully short, but time as well; the blockade held up the preparations and the lost barrel staves were virtually irreplaceable in the time available. This, in fact, was probably Drake's most effective contribution to the failure of the Armada.

Meanwhile the preparations were continuing, albeit, thanks to Drake, a little more slowly than had been hoped. In addition to barrels for holding provisions, there were pottery containers of all sorts both for storing and eating. An estimate of 100,000 pieces of pottery – plates, small bowls, pots and jugs – all of glazed earthenware, had been assessed for the 1586 version of the Armada, to be produced by factories in Seville and Lisbon. From the pottery recovered from Armada wrecks, Colin Martin has established that it probably was these very factories that supplied the basic mess-equipment for the Armada of 1588, although on a considerably smaller scale. A few intact samples have survived among the material recovered from *La Trinidad Valencera*: two small, rather crudely made, plates, about 200mm in diameter, a small green-glazed bowl, rather like a porringer; and a little green-glazed jug with a simple loop-handle and a pinched spout. In addition, of course, there are numerous sherds or fragments from all the Armada wreck-sites. As well as pottery mess-dishes there are, in the manifest of *La Trinidad Valencera*, references to items of wood: '80 wooden plates; 44 wooden bowls', though there does not appear to be any reference to wooden spoons, such as that recovered from *La Trinidad Valencera* to accompany the wooden bowl also found (Cat 9.64–9.65). In addition large storage vessels were required for some commodities, such as olive oil and vinegar. From the wrecks of *La Trinidad Valencera*, the *Girona* and the *Santa Maria de la Rosa* came fragments of such containers and, fortunately, from *La Trinidad Valencera* two complete examples (Cat 8.1–8.2). These, known as 'olive jars', have a capacity of about 6.25 litres, almost exactly half of the Castilian arroba in which the supplies of oil and vinegar were accounted. Surprisingly, while it might be thought that 'dry' provisions would be packed in sacks, the *La Trinidad Valencera* olive jar in fact contained lentils when it was found. Colin Martin has calculated that *La Trinidad Valencera* would have required 758 such jars to contain her share of the 10,000 arrobas of oil and the 21,000 arrobas of vinegar issued to the entire fleet. The number so far accounted for from the wreck is only 11, a very small proportion of the assumed total. In the manifest there is, incidentally, a reference to 'sacks of hemp for changing the biscuit', possibly because the original sacks had been damaged.

In the inventories of *La Trinidad Valencera*, preserved in the Spanish archives, are entries relating to the foodstuffs and other items actually loaded. Much of this, of course, is likely to have been consumed in port, before the Armada sailed. It does, however, reflect the enormous quantities of food involved and the huge costs of the provisioning. There was a daily menu laid down for the men: 1.5lb of biscuit, 3/10 of a pint of wine and 2 gallons of water a day; on Sundays and Thursdays they were to get 6oz of bacon and 2oz rice; on Mondays and Wednesdays 6oz of bone and 3oz of dried beans or peas; and on Tuesdays, Fridays and Saturdays 6oz of tuna with oil and vinegar, or dried, cod or octopus, or, instead, 5 sardines and 3oz of chick peas. This adds up to some 23,000 calories per man per week, which, interestingly, is nearly 4,000 more than what was laid down by the Merchant Shipping Act of 1894 for steerage passengers. That the rations had to be weighed out, according to the regulations, is suggested by the items listed in *La Trinidad Valencera*'s inventory, by actual finds from the wrecks and by the instruction issued by Medina Sidonia that the troops were not 'to go down and take or choose their rations by force'. In the inventory are several items for measuring or weighing: '3 wooden measures for wine or water'; '2 large wooden buckets for measuring wine; 9 smaller wooden buckets for measuring water' and even '2 wooden measures for measuring ordinary wine; one wooden measure for measuring Candian wine'. For measuring out dry goods there appear in the manifest several references to weighing equipment: 'one Roman balance with its weight; 2 pairs of balances'; 'a set of scales with their steel arm and brass balances'. From the wreck-site of *La Trinidad Valencera* came 2 steelyards and

2 steelyard weights, while the *Girona* produced one steelyard weight (Cat 8.10). It is probable that the various pestles and mortars found on board *La Trinidad Valencera* may have been used in the preparation of foodstuffs, or possibly drugs and medicines: the large bronze one rather resembles examples known as apothecaries' mortars.

The lists of actual foodstuffs are prodigious:

Biscuit: 1,858 quintals and 61 lbs
White biscuit: 6 quintals
Fresh bread: 5,618 lbs
Fresh mutton: 992 lbs
Fresh pork: 3,664 lbs
Salt beef: 108 lbs
Salt sardines: 6,135
Sardines of Setuba: 6,000
Fresh beef: 9,019 lbs
Rice: 96 quintals and 83 lbs
Beans: 261 fanegas
Beans: 221 fanegas
Bacon: 133 quintals and 5 lbs
Cheese: 48 quintals and 50 lbs
Codfish: 25 quintals
Octopus: 8 quintals
Salt: 42 fanegas

This is just one group of consecutive entries, interspersed with quantities of liquid provisions:

Wine of Candia: 696 almudes and 4 canadas
Wine: 8,894 arrobas
Vinegar: 542 arrobas
Oil: 346 arrobas

To make matters worse for both the accounting officer and the historian, several different measuring systems were in use at the same time. For the dry goods some of the items, the biscuit, for example, and the mutton, beef and salt pork, are accounted in Castilian measure; other items, including the salt, in Portuguese measure. The same is true for liquids.

Despite Drake's unfriendly action in destroying the barrel-staves, one load of water consisted of '256 pipes full of water, with 1,009 hoops' – that is, some 28,160 gallons of water. Another reference is to '32 wooden barrels, with 4 iron hoops, for water'. The likelihood is that many of these barrels were of unseasoned timber, which resulted in much of the water going bad. Whether of seasoned or unseasoned timber, a number of barrel-staves have survived from *La Trinidad Valencera* (Cat 8.4), although that particular barrel actually had contained gunpowder.

Among the debris on all the wreck-sites were animal-bones, the remains, for the most part, of meals inadequately tidied away. Among those found on the *Santa Maria de la Rosa*, on the site of the galley fire, were those of sheep, cattle and chickens. The last-named may have come from birds carried live on board as was frequently done, although there is no mention of chicken among the official menus or in the inventory. There is a reference in an account of a crossing from Salamanca in Spain to Mexico in 1554 to a bishop on board having the forethought to bring with him a coop of chickens.

Other finds from *La Trinidad Valencera* include several pine-cones, the seeds of which were eaten, presumably to vary the diet a little, as well as several bay-leaves. From the *Girona*, too, came a small token of diet-variation – a plum-stone (Cat 8.25).

Other items of equipment which had to be ordered, paid for and loaded were almost infinite. There are, inevitably, many references to lighting equipment: '6 glazed lamps to give light to the soldiers', '8 wooden lanterns, 4 furnished with linen, the others with horn covers', as well as '6 arrobas of candles'. Of the lantern types, two are represented among the equipment recovered from *La Trinidad Valencera*: of one of these only the lid survives; of the other the base, the lid and three of the side-members, grooved to receive the glass or horn shields, have survived along with the little pewter candle-holder (Cat 9.30). One rather intriguing find from *La Trinidad Valencera* is a small brush or whisk of straw, implying a rather domestic aspect of ship-keeping.

Not all the supplies and stores, of course, consisted of domestic necessities. Among the items recovered from the *Girona* was a very large quantity of lead, for making shot, and also pieces of copper, which may be ingots for use on board. From *La Trinidad Valencera* came a lump of pine-resin, (Cat 8.17) which may have been used for making varnishes for water-proofing. It would appear from the manifest that *La Trinidad Valencera* was carrying a quite incredible quantity of resin, amounting to several tons. There are also, as listed in the manifest, spare-parts of all descriptions, including those for gun-carriages, like the unused felloe from a wheel.

Sources used for Chapter 8

Arnold, J.B., and Weddle, R.S., *The Nautical Archaeology of Padre Island*, London, 1978

Flanagan, L., 'Steelyards and Steelyard-weights', *International J. Nautical Archaeol.*, (16.4) 1987

Flanagan, L., Martin, C. and Stenuit, R., *Tresors de l'Armada*, Brussels, 1985

Lewis, M., *The Spanish Armada*, London, 1960
Martin, C., *Full Fathom Five*, London, 1975
Martin, C., 'Spanish Armada Pottery', *International J. Nautical Archeol*, (8.4)
    1979
Stenuit, R., *Treasures of the Armada*, London, 1974
Walker, B., *The Armada*, Amsterdam, 1982

Victualling and Provisions

8.1 OLIVE JAR, Pottery
300mm h
Globular or ovoid pottery container,
unglazed,with round bottom and
short collared neck. The belly has
parallel grooves. While these pottery
containers are known as 'olive' jars
and, indeed, were used for olive oil,
vinegar and even wine on a regular
basis, this one contained lentils
when found. Such a vessel has a
capacity of about six and a quarter
litres – almost exactly half of a
Castilian arroba
La Trinidad Valencera

8.2 OLIVE JAR, Pottery
310mm h
As above; this one is cracked but
not smashed, despite the fact that
she lay under one of the *La Trinidad
Valencera*'s anchors
La Trinidad Valencera

8.3 OLIVE JAR, Pottery
180mm+ h
A large fragment of a jar similar to
the above
La Trinidad Valencera

8.4 BARREL STAVES, Wood
605mm l
Nine staves of a wooden barrel, all
about 10mm thick; there are two
widths, narrow and wide, the latter
being about 31mm at the centre,
narrowing to about 24mm at the
ends. All are grooved at each end to
receive the top and bottom covers of
the barrel
La Trinidad Valencera

8.5 BASES OF STAVE-BUILT CONTAINERS, Wood
134mm d
Two flat circular sheets of wood,
with a mean thickness of about 8mm
La Trinidad Valencera

8.6 STEELYARD, Bronze
520mm l
Square-sectioned bar of bronze,
turned into a flat tongue at one end,
with three square perforations and
two lugs at that end, which has a
forked decorated terminal
La Trinidad Valencera

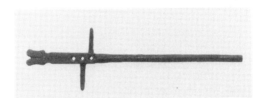

8.7 STEELYARD WEIGHT, Lead and Copper
115mm h; 3.3kg +
Globular footed weight of lead, with
a collar at the top from which
springs a semi-hexagonal suspension
loop. The surface is covered with
thin copper sheeting, of which a part
survives
La Trinidad Valencera

8.8 STEELYARD WEIGHT, Lead and Copper
165mm h; 6.51kg
As above, but much larger
La Trinidad Valencera

8.9 STEELYARD, Bronze

275mm+ l

Light bar of square-sectioned
bronze, with one end flattened in
which are two surviving square holes
and half of another, at which point
the bar has broken; at this end there
are also two lugs
La Trinidad Valencera

8.10 STEELYARD WEIGHT, Lead and Copper

105mm+ h; 4kg+

Pear-shaped lead weight with flat
base and short neck; the suspension
loop for fitting on the beam of the
steelyard (or 'Roman' balance) is
missing. Covered with fine copper
sheeting, about half of which
survives
Girona

8.11 NESTING WEIGHT, Bronze

41mm d; 77.30g

Small straight-sided circular cup of
bronze; there are two parallel lines
on the inside below the rim and a
cross roughly inscribed on the
bottom. This should be one of the
larger of a set of about eight, fitting
inside one another, the largest
having a lid, often fitted with a
scale-beam
La Trinidad Valencera

8.12 NESTING WEIGHT, Bronze

24mm d; 12.79g

As above, but with three lines on
the upper edge of the rim and a
crossed 'N' on the interior of the
base. It is unlikely that the two
belonged to the same set as there
would not be sufficient space for the
four intermediate weights
La Trinidad Valencera

8.13 PESTLE, Bronze
214mm l
Symmetrical round bronze bar with
central knop, expanding gently in
both directions and ending in a pear
shape (see colour plate)
La Trinidad Valencera

8.14 MORTAR, Bronze
94mm h
Circular container of heavy bronze,
with a slight foot at the base and a
rounded interior bottom. Four lugs
are fitted at the four quarters on the
outside, each with three crests. One
side has been slightly crushed which
has caused a slight crack (see colour
plate)
La Trinidad Valencera

8.15 MORTAR, Stone
118mm h
Round container with straight sides
and three projecting columns on the
outside; the inside has been carved
in a cup shape, with a round
bottom; part of one side has been
damaged
La Trinidad Valencera

8.16 PESTLE, Bronze
213mm l
Cylindrical bar of bronze with a
central knop from which it swells
gently to form a flattened pear-
shaped 'working' end; the handle-
end terminates in a collar
surmounted by a round knop and
point
Girona

8.17 BLOCK, Resin
360mm w; 4.2kg
Block of resin more or less oval;
covered with cortex; chipped
recently in one or two places
La Trinidad Valencera

8.18 INGOT, Lead
675mm l; 53kg
Lead boat-shaped triangular-
sectioned ingot; on one face the
Roman numeral IIII V is stamped,
and in addition four other stamps
apparently representing four conjoint
squares. One of 29 such ingots or
parts thereof on the *Girona*
Girona

8.19 INGOT, Lead
670mm l; 58kg
As above, but stamped X III
Girona

8.20 INGOT (?), Copper
234mm l; 1.05kg
Flat cast plate of copper, straight-
sided in the middle, expanding at
the ends
Girona

8.21 INGOT (?), Copper
274mm l; 1.98kg
As above, but embedded in
concretion at one end, where it
appears to have a circular-sectioned
hook, possibly for suspension
Girona

8.22 PINE CONE, Vegetable matter
71mm h
Cone of *Pinus pinea*, some of the
seeds, which were eaten as a diet-
supplement, still in place
La Trinidad Valencera

8.23 BRAZIL NUT, Vegetable matter
52mm l
Triquetrous seed of *Bertholettia
excelsa*; the shell is cracked and the
seed presumably eaten
Santa Maria de la Rosa

8.24 BAY LEAF, Vegetable matter
45mm l
Leaf of *Laurus nobilis* used to flavour
food
La Trinidad Valencera

8.25 PLUM STONE, Vegetable matter
15mm l
Seed of *Prunus sp.*, now embedded
in concretion
Girona

CHAPTER 9
Life on Board

While life on board any sixteenth-century sailing ship, particularly on one at sea for any length of time, cannot have been enjoyable, it must have been considerably worse for Armada crews. In the first place the duration of the voyage had been prolonged beyond expectation; the campaign was victualled for six months and was presumably scheduled to last six months, either up to or including the invasion of England, or the failure of the expedition. Many of the crews must have been aboard their ships for some months before the fleet even sailed. There then followed the abortive first leg of the voyage, in which three weeks were spent zig-zagging in atrocious weather from Lisbon to La Coruna; in the course of this, as the Duke of Medina Sidonia reported to the King, water had turned rotten in the barrels, there was a serious shortage of provisions, many of the men were ill – some with contagious diseases – and many of the ships were damaged as a result of 'squalls the like of which have never been seen before'. The experience had been so bad for many of the men that the Duke wrote to the King:

> I have posted guards at all the landing stages and on all the roads by which the men might try to escape . . . Water, which has been my greatest worry, is being loaded as carefully as possible. I have twenty-six coopers working day and night to repair the casks which were completely wrecked in the storm . . .I have continued to give the men fresh meat, but not bread, as there is not enough, even for the sick . . . Only nine have died, thanks be to God.

Even on a peaceful crossing of the Atlantic in the sixteenth century, life was not often enjoyable; in a description of a voyage from Spain to Mexico in 1554 Tomas de la Torre describes the ship in which he was travelling as 'a narrow prison, very strong, from which nobody can escape even though there are neither bars nor chains, and it is so cruel that no distinction is made among the prisoners, who are all treated and punished alike. The crowded space, the suffocating air and the heat are unbearable. The deck is usually the bed.' Moreover 'the place is full of lice that eat every living creature, and one cannot wash one's clothes, as they shrink when cleaned in sea-water'. The only differences likely in an Armada ship were that some of the 'prisoners' were actually in chains – at the oars of the galleys and galleasses – that the crowding was almost certainly more severe and that often, as an alternative to intense heat, there was intense cold. In addition, universally, there was sea-sickness. 'Shortly,' says la Torre, 'the sea made us understand that it was no place for human habitation . . . Some were below deck being boiled alive, others were being roasted by the sun above deck; cast on the deck, stepped on and trampled, dirty beyond words.' Add to these discomforts the knowledge that the vessel is built of highly inflammable materials; that it is carrying gunpowder; and that sometime, someone is going to try blasting it out of the sea – and the inmates with it: the fact that its own crew may be trying to do the same to the other ship comes as scant consolation.

This, then, was the background to life on board ship in the sixteenth century. If the rations officially allocated actually survived and were, in due course, served up,the occupants would not die of starvation. Theoretically, at least, they would get enough to eat and drink. The ordinary soldiers and sailors aboard would have their rations duly weighed or measured out for them by their officers and the ship's crew and eat them off their standard-issue earthenware plates and bowls (Cat 9.72–9.74) or wooden bowls (Cat 9.64). No doubt their wine would be measured into similar earthenware jugs (Cat 9.71) from a wine-skin of the type recovered from *La Trinidad Valencera* – which, unfortunately, it was impossible to conserve and only the top and stopper of one survive (Cat 9.93).

For the officers and noblemen on board, however, life was obviously a little different. Presumably the weather, disease and sea-sickness were constants that none could avoid totally and it is likely also that the allocation of essentials such as water and food was carried out in a fairly egalitarian fashion. However, the receptacles for these items differed between ranks, with those accustomed to high quality wares still using them even on board ship.

The range of pewter tableware recovered from all the Irish Armada wrecks constitutes probably the greatest and most varied range of sixteenth-century pewter tableware of fixed date extant. The selection from *La Trinidad Valencera* in particular is spectacular: bowls, dishes, plates of all sizes; jugs, beakers, goblets, flagons and candle-holders of a variety that is quite breathtaking. Since it includes a number of marked pieces, some possibly Spanish and Flemish and some, certainly, English, it assumes an importance that cannot be exaggerated. Included, for example, are two plates (Cat 9.8, 9.15) bearing the touch-mark of Edward Roe – the letters 'E R' on either side of a Tudor Rose. At first sight, this gives the impression that the plates might have belonged to Elizabeth of England herself, perhaps not just a modern error, for on one of the pieces an attempt has been made to obliterate the Tudor Rose with a punch, causing a great depression in the rim of the plate. It is, however, simply the maker's touch-mark; he had been Master of the London Company of Pewterers in 1582 and was again, as it happens, in 1588.

Presumably, therefore, these plates, imported from one of the craftsmen, had a certain cachet. Beside the touch are the initials of the owner, 'JZ'. Colin Martin has tentatively identified the initials as being those of Juan Zapota, whose son, Sebastien, is listed as being on board *La Trinidad Valencera* when she sailed. Several other items bear the touches of pewterers as yet unidentified.

A number of other pieces of pewter-ware bear the names or initials of their owners. Those plates which were crucial in identifying the wreck of the *Santa Maria de la Rosa* have their owner's name written out in full: 'Matute' (Cat 9.9), for Francisco Ruiz Matute. The testimony of the unfortunate thrice-interrogated Giovanni gave the first clue, for in the transcript of his second interrogation is recorded: 'He saith the Captain of this ship was Villafranca of San Sebastian, and Matuta was Captain of the Infanterie'. So the witness of the 'lonely frightened boy' proved vital to the excavators in reassuring them that their wreck was the one they hoped it was. And, indeed, confirmation of the boy's testimony was found in the muster-rolls drawn up by the Duke of Medina Sidonia just before the Armada sailed; Francisco Ruiz Matute is, indeed, shown to have embarked with his ninety-five soldiers of the crack Sicilian tercio of Don Diego de Pimental on the *Santa Maria de la Rosa*.

Other plates, dishes and bowls, unfortunately, while bearing their owners' marks, carry them in a fashion that was probably of doubtful value as a means of identification even for their owners in 1588. One, again from the *Santa Maria de la Rosa*, bears what seem to be the letters 'AL'; even if this helped 'AL[onso]' to identify his plate it certainly is of no assistance to the twentieth-century archaeologist.Others have 'O', or 'X', or even 'A' by itself, while still others display simple geometric designs.

More luxurious even than the pewter is the range of silver-ware recovered, almost exclusively from the *Girona*. This monopoly is perhaps not totally surprising when we recall that on the *Girona*, when she sank at Lacada Point, Co. Antrim, were crowded some 1,300 people; some were survivors of two previous wrecks and included among them Don Alonso de Leiva and his retinue. We know that de Leiva was travelling in some style; he is known to have entertained the Duke on board his first command, *La Rata Sancta Maria Encoronada*, before the Armada eventually sailed from Lisbon. As Robert Stenuit says: 'he received him in grand style, with musical accompaniment, at his table sumptuously set with silver plate and cutlery and gold-plated candelabra (which I found four centuries later).' Unfortunately, however, the silver plate has not survived four hundred years under the corrosive waters of the Atlantic anything like as well as the pewter, some of which had enjoyed the incalculable advantage of being totally buried in sand on the more sheltered site of *La Trinidad Valencera*. As much as possible must be reconstructed from the more solid pieces among the many hundreds of flimsy fragments. Without doubt among the more solid pieces are the jug-spouts, of a type well known in the late sixteenth-century, usually, but not always, attached to heavy silver jugs. One of these has decoration in the form of a grotesque mask (Cat 9.33), a relatively common motif; another is much simpler and has stylised plant ornament (Cat 9.34).

Among the more fragmented pieces are plates with typical Renaissance-style plant, scroll and strapwork decoration (Cat 9.36), as well as a part of the base of what must be an impressive dish, the base itself being some 150mm in diameter. Rim fragments of a silver-gilt dish again suggest an impressive original, some 750mm in diameter,the edge decorated with simple ridges. A succession of other feet, finials and fragments (Cat 9.40) lend confirmation to Stenuit's description of the grand style in which de Leiva, using this very table-ware, entertained the Duke. One of the frustrating factors in attempting to reconstruct from these varied fragments the shapes and styles of the original vessels is that practically all of the sixteenth-century Spanish silver plate otherwise surviving is ecclesiastical, so that parallels are difficult to find.

Some items, however, are not difficult to identify or reconstruct, incomplete though they are. One example is the range of silver taper- and candle-sticks which have been preserved to a greater or lesser degree. Nearly a dozen of these survive, all of similar design: simple balusters with a cylindrical holder at the top into which the candle fitted (Cat 9.46–9.50); none of the bases, unfortunately, has survived. One passing observation is that the standardisation of the candlesticks seems to have been as loose as the standardisation of ordnance calibres; no two of the silver candle-sticks are for the same thickness of candle. Attention is inevitably drawn to the inherent danger of the use of candles in such holders on a ship at sea and to the grave responsibility shouldered by the boatswain.

One aspect of the finds from the *Girona* that is quite extraordinary is the range of table-forks, which, again, constitute one of the most varied and complete collections of early table-forks in Europe. Among the *Girona* collection are forks with two, three, four, or five prongs or tynes (Cat 9.57–9.60). The variety of handles is also unparalleled; there are many in the form of horses' hooves, with grotesque human torsoes, terminals in the form of a serpent and in the form of a club or fleur-de-lys (Cat 9.54–9.56).Unfortunately only one, with two prongs and a horse's foot terminal (Cat 9.52) is virtually complete. Surviving examples of sixteenth-century table-forks are not common and a group of this size and variety, so closely dated, is without parallel.

Probably more a souvenir than a practical item of table-ware is the little cast and spun bowl bearing a representation of St James (Santiago) in armour on horseback and brandishing a sword, dated 'ANNO 1583', made in commemoration of the victory of Alexander de Bazan, Marquis of Santa Cruz, at

Terceira (Cat 9.51). Another of these commemorative pieces, in better condition, is preserved in Antwerp. It is particularly appropriate that such a piece should appear on an Armada ship, reminding us that Santa Cruz was the original inventor of the Armada.

A surprising piece recovered is the blue and white decorated bowl of Chinese porcelain of the Ming or Wan Li dynasties (Cat 9.70). Naturally enough Spain had trading contacts with the Far East, not only because of her Pacific colonies, but also through the longer-established and more traditional overland routes culminating in Venice, the great trading and entrepôt port of the Mediterranean. Whatever its means of arriving on *La Trinidad Valencera* it must, even then, have been regarded as highly valuable and must have belonged to one of the wealthier officers or noblemen on board. Its preservation through a shipwreck and 400 years under the sea is quite miraculous.

Whether the more simple copper dishes, bowls and candlesticks are more closely associated with the earthenware and wooden mess-equipment of the lower decks is not certain. It does, however, seem reasonable to suppose that the simple wooden spoons (Cat 9.65) and the rather crudely fashioned knives (Cat 9.66–9.67) are. It is less easy to establish the social status of what seem to be salt-cellars (Cat 9.69), once thought to be gaming-cups and thereby, apparently, embodying a gentle contravention of Medina Sidonia's moral directives.

The lack of sanitation on board a sixteenth-century ship is a well-established fact. Disposal of waste-products, human or animal, was either directly or eventually over the side of the ship. This, of course, tended to be impracticable in even moderately rough weather and so they, and the remains of meals, tended to be washed down into the hold and accumulate on the ballast. This was also the area where the cooking was done on an open fire. To judge by the evidence from the *Santa Maria de la Rosa*, the galley fire was not even accorded the bespoke brick-built structure known from the earlier English *Mary Rose*. This was also the area where the crew generally had to sleep in rough weather. It is not altogether surprising, therefore, that in addition to deficiency diseases, such as scurvy (the important role of citrus fruits and their vitamin C content had not, of course, been recognised), diseases resulting from a total lack of hygiene were also rampant. Fastidious officers and gentlemen on the *Girona*, where the problem was aggravated by the presence of slaves chained to their benches at the oars, availed themselves of little silver scent-bottles, with tiny crystal droppers, in an attempt to disguise or, at least, alleviate the appalling stench that must have been all-pervasive (Cat 9.75–9.78). In view of the observations about the omnivorous lice on transatlantic voyages, which must have been at least as great a problem on Armada ships, the presence and constant use of fine-toothed combs (Cat 9.80) is not at all surprising.

Shipboard medicine and surgery is quite well attested in the sixteenth-century. From the *Mary Rose*, of 1545, came a whole array of the Barber-Surgeon's equipment, found in his cabin on the starboard side of the main gundeck. At the time of the *Mary Rose* this man filled the role of barber, surgeon, physician, apothecary and, presumably, dentist. In a chest in this cabin were found nine lidded wooden canisters containing ointments and peppercorns (a popular treatment for agues and quinsies). In addition were found two syringes and the handles of several instruments whose steel blades had totally disappeared. There were also a large brass shaving bowl and a small bleeding bowl. Not in the chest, but elsewhere in the cabin were a small brazier and a heavy mortar for grinding drugs; possibly *La Trinidad Valencera*'s mortar (Cat 8.14) also had this use.

Quite a lot is known about Spanish sea-born medicine; a complete list of medical supplies is available from a transatlantic voyage by a Spanish ship in 1549. It includes items of equipment like syringes, mortars, spatulas, fine-scales, sheets for bandages and plaster of Paris, as well as a whole range of drugs – powders, pills and ointments, of some hundred different kinds, many of them of American origin. It may well be, therefore, that the nesting-weights from *La Trinidad Valencera* (Cat 8.11–8.12) may have had a role to fill in the medicine chest.

The only other items from the Irish Armada wrecks likely to have medical connections are the tweezers from the *Girona* (Cat 9.81), possibly for extracting splinters, and two ceramic drug-jars from *La Trinidad Valencera*, though what they contained can never be firmly deduced. Perhaps the larger was for pills of some kind, the smaller for an ointment. They have both been so well scoured by the sea over 400 years that no attempt at analysis of contents would be feasible. It is possible that the end of a wooden box or chest recovered (Cat 9.89) might have served as a medicine chest.

Fishing over the side is quite frequently attested as a means of providing supplements to and variations from the provisions on board, so the lead fishing-weights from the *Girona* (Cat 9.87) are not at all surprising. Indeed Valeriano de Manzera, master of the ship *Nuestra Senora de la Concepcion* in 1552, carried on board a large box with padlock and bound with iron straps, containing a small rowboat for fishing as well as anglers' gear.

For amusement on board, whenever the men might find the time, the space, the energy or the inclination, one or two objects have been recovered. One is the neck of some guitar-like stringed instrument (Cat 9.84), which seems to have had up to 26 strings, or at least grooves made by such a number – it is impossible to state precisely how many it had. It certainly does not seem to be a suitable 'martial' instrument, to join the fifes and drums we hear of inspiring the ship's own crew or striking fear into the enemy. Nor does it seem particularly suitable for liturgical use. The tambourine recovered (Cat 9.85) again seems more recreational than either martial or devotional. The small wooden balls recovered (Cat 9.88) suggest there was occasionally space and time for some simple ball-game.

Other miscellaneous personal belongings discovered on the wreck-site include: the little hexagonal box (Cat 9.94) from *La Trinidad Valencera*, no longer thought to be the two ends of a concertina; two little bronze keys from the *Girona*, presumably used for locking some container for objects of value, whether jewellery, drugs or money; and a small cage from *La Trinidad Valencera* (Cat 9.86) perhaps for a small bird. It is most unlikely it was for the rat whose skeleton was also recovered from the wreck-site.

Sources used for Chapter 9

Arnold, J., and Weddle, R.S., *The Nautical Archaeology of Padre Island*, London, 1978
Flanagan, L., Martin, C. and Stenuit, R., *Tresors de l'Armada*, Brussels, 1985
Martin, C., *Full Fathom Five*, London, 1975
Oman, C., *The Golden Age of Spanish Silver*, London, 1968
Rule, M., *The Mary Rose*, London, 1982
Stenuit, R., *Treasures of the Armada*, London, 1974

Life on Board

9.1 LARGE BOWL, Pewter
353mm d
Large round pewter bowl, 82mm deep, with curved sides; flat rim with pewterer's mark on underside (unidentified)
La Trinidad Valencera

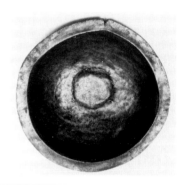

9.2 LARGE BOWL, Pewter
335mm+ d
As above, except that only a quarter of the rim survives and has a raised edge
La Trinidad Valencera

9.3 LARGE DISH, Pewter
354mm d
Large round pewter dish with wide
flat rim, with engraved linear
decoration and concentric circles in
the centre; slight tears at the angles
La Trinidad Valencera

9.4 LARGE DISH, Pewter
309mm d
As above but without decoration
La Trinidad Valencera

9.5 LARGE DISH, Pewter
287mm d
As above but with two conjoint
lozenges on underside of rim
La Trinidad Valencera

9.6 LARGE PLATE, Pewter
291mm d
Large round pewter plate with wide
flat rim; badly damaged and with
several holes; pewterer's mark on
underside of rim (unidentified)
La Trinidad Valencera

9.7 LARGE PLATE, Pewter
360mm d
As above, but even more badly
damaged; on the underside of the
rim is inscribed 'AL'(?)
Santa Maria de la Rosa

9.8 PLATE, Pewter
257mm d
Round pewter plate with wide flat
rim and circular decoration in the
centre. On the top and underside of
the rim are English pewterer's
marks, with a Rose, of Edward Roe,
Master of the London Company of
Pewterers in 1582 and 1588 and the
owner's initials 'JZ' for Juan Zapota,
whose son, Sebastian, was on board
La Trinidad Valencera

9.9 PLATES, Pewter
202mm d
A pair of round pewter plates with
flat rims; on the underside of each
rim is the inscription 'Matute' for
Francisco Ruiz Matute who was a
Captain of Infantry on board; the
finding of these plates positively
identified the wreck
Santa Maria de la Rosa

9.10 PLATE, Pewter
217mm d
Round pewter plate with flat rim
La Trinidad Valencera

9.11 PLATE, Pewter
213mm d
As above, but with holes
La Trinidad Valencera

9.12 PLATE, Pewter
205mm d
Round pewter plate with decoration
of radial lines; holed in several
places
La Trinidad Valencera

9.13 PLATE, Pewter
203mm d
As above
La Trinidad Valencera

9.14 PLATE, Pewter
205mm d
As above, but with traces of an
indecipherable inscription under the
rim and on the rim a scratched 'T' (?)
La Trinidad Valencera

9.15 PLATE, Pewter
203mm d
Round, and rather flat, pewter plate
with an unidentified stamp under
the rim and the stamp of Edward
Roe (and of Juan Zapota) with the
Tudor Rose defaced on the upper
surface
La Trinidad Valencera

9.16 PLATE, Pewter
215mm d
Round and quite deep pewter plate
with flat beaded rim; an unidentified
pewterer's mark under the rim
La Trinidad Valencera

9.17 PLATE, Pewter
208mm d
Round pewter plate with flat rim, on
the top of which is an unidentified
pewterer's mark; underneath is an
'O'
La Trinidad Valencera

9.18 PLATE, Pewter
203mm d
Round, rather deep, pewter plate
with flat rim, of which two-thirds
survives
Girona

9.19 DISH, Pewter
131mm d
Small round dish with straight sides
and a raised area in the centre;
everted rim
La Trinidad Valencera

9.20 BOWL, Pewter
131mm d
Round pewter bowl with straight
sides and beaded rim; of otherwise
indecipherable inscriptions on the
base only an 'X' can now be
discerned
La Trinidad Valencera

9.21 BOWL, Pewter
127mm d
Round pewter bowl with curved
sides and beaded rim; several holes.
There is an accidental scratch on the
bottom, where an 'A' seems to be
inscribed
La Trinidad Valencera

9.22 BEAKER, Pewter
89mm h
Small pewter beaker with straight
sides, in the shape of a flower-pot.
Several small holes and tears
La Trinidad Valencera

9.23 BEAKER, Pewter
98mm h
As above
La Trinidad Valencera

9.24 GOBLET, Pewter
133mm h
Round straight-sided cup on a little
stand and stepped foot
La Trinidad Valencera

9.25 FLAGON, Pewter
177mm h
Globular-bodied flagon on flared
foot, with four pairs of parallel lines
decorating the body. The neck
constricts and has a beaded rim of
which only a small portion survives
La Trinidad Valencera

9.26 JUG, Pewter
174mm h
Straight-sided jug with rounded
bottom on short stand and flared
foot; curved spout and swan-neck
handle
La Trinidad Valencera

9.27 SALT-CELLAR(?), Pewter
112mm w
Triangular pewter receptacle with
folded rim and circular depression in
centre
La Trinidad Valencera

9.28 LID, Pewter
85mm h
Round domed pewter lid with
central conical handle; several holes
La Trinidad Valencera

9.29 SPOON, Pewter
175mm l
Pewter spoon with fiddle-shaped
bowl and rat-tail handle
La Trinidad Valencera

9.30 CANDLE-HOLDER, Pewter
75mm d
Circular pewter candle-holder
consisting of a little tube whose
inside diameter is 33mm, mounted
on a domed foot with a little flange;
a series of pewterer's marks
(unidentified) on the base
La Trinidad Valencera

9.31 CANDLE-HOLDERS, Pewter
70mm d
As above but without marks
La Trinidad Valencera

9.32 SPOUTED DISH, Pewter
290mm w
Round pewter bowl, 188mm in diameter, on a short stand with a wide flared foot; an open spout 87mm long projects from one side; opposite is a loop carrying a loose ring. When found it was badly crushed and its shape then suggested it might have been a pap-dish for feeding invalids
La Trinidad Valencera

9.33 JUG-SPOUT, Silver
87mm l; 115.75g
Spout from a jug cast in the form of a grotesque human mask with luxuriant beard
Girona

9.34 JUG-SPOUT, Silver-gilt
50mm l; 70.14g
As above, but broken and with stylised plant ornament
Girona

9.35 PLATE-FRAGMENT, Silver
75mm w; 14.45g
Fragment of a highly decorated
silver plate with formalised plant
ornament
Girona

9.36 PLATE-FRAGMENT,
Silver-gilt
77mm w; 19.63g
As above but with scroll and
strapwork
Girona

9.37 PLATE-FRAGMENT, Silver
49mm w; 6.26g
Small fragment of plate with fleur-
de-lys at edge
Girona

9.38 PLATE-FRAGMENT, Silver
37mm w; 4.21g
Small fragment of plate with plant
decorations
Girona

9.39 DISH-FRAGMENT, Silver
104mm l; 28.24g
Portion of the base-ring of a silver
dish, decorated on the outside with
geometric decoration; the dish would
have had a base-diameter of some
150mm
Girona

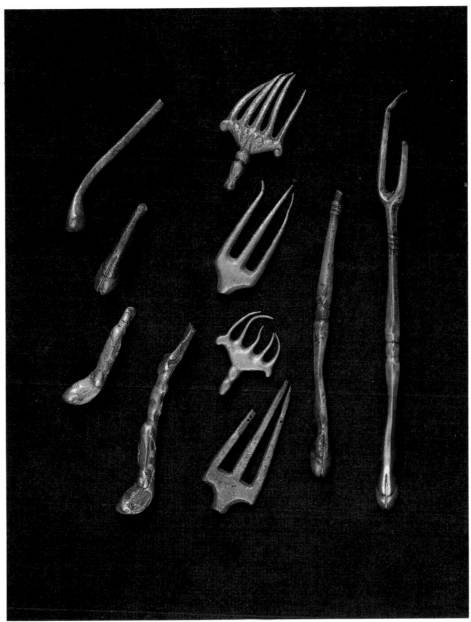

9.52–9.57 and 9.59 A selection of Silver Forks from the *Girona*. Note the terminals in the form of an animal hoof and of serpents, and at the top that of a club

10.1–10.4 Hollow Gold Buttons from four sets from the *Girona*, most with attachment loops intact. Decoration is in low relief, with cross-hatching and various motifs

9.40 DISH-FRAGMENTS,
Silver-gilt
185mm l; 16.21g
Two fragments of the rim of a dish,
decorated with concentric grooves
and ridges; the dish would have had
a diameter of some 750mm
Girona

9.41 DOLPHIN, Silver
25mm l; 6.19g
Small cast silver dolphin, possibly
the finial from the lid of a tankard
Girona

9.42 LION-MASKS, Silver
37mm h; 30.20g
A pair of small cast lion-masks with
suspension loops at the top, possibly
handle-mountings; badly abraded
Girona

9.43 HANDLE, Silver
43mm h; 19.43g
Simple scroll handle, detached from
a dish or cup
Girona

9.44 FOOT, Silver
35mm h; 18.17g
The rear leg of an animal, cast in
silver, the detached foot of a dish of
some sort
Girona

9.45 FINIAL, Silver
49mm l; 34.06g
Solid cast finial, in the form of a
dolphin or other sea-creature
Girona

9.46 TAPER-STICK, Silver
95mm h; 72.77g
Small baluster-shaped taper-stick
with a holder of 12mm diameter,
with a solid threaded projection at
the bottom for attachment to a base
now missing
Girona

9.47 TAPER-STICK, Silver
72mm h; 61.18g
As above, but lacking the holder and
with a hollow threaded projection
for attachment to the base now
missing
Girona

9.48 CANDLE-STICKS, Silver
135mm h; 262.87g (average)
Pair of baluster-shaped candlesticks
with holders of 28mm in diameter;
the bases are missing
Girona

9.49 CANDLE-STICK, Silver
83mm h; 166.67g
Top of heavy silver candle-stick of
baluster shape, with holder of 25mm
diameter
Girona

9.50 CANDLE-STICK, Silver
47mm h; 80.27g
Holder of candle-stick similar to
above, with provision for a candle of
23mm diameter
Girona

9.51 BOWL, Casting-metal
124mm d
Small, rather shallow bowl, with
slightly domed bottom. In the centre
of the inside is a low-relief
representation of a man on
horseback riding from right to left,
brandishing a sword in his right
hand. Around the figure is the
inscription *ANNO 1583 +
PATRIAE. ET. AM(ICITIAE)*
(For fatherland and friendship). The
inscription is set in an ornament in
the form of a crown and the rest of
the inside is decorated with void
oval-pattern. This is one of a series
of dishes made to commemorate the
victory of the Marquis of Santa Cruz
at Terceira in 1583
La Trinidad Valencera

9.52 FORK, Silver
139mm l; 15.70g
Two-pronged fork with baluster
stem and terminal in the form of a
hoof (see colour plate)
Girona

9.53 FORK-HANDLES, Silver
37–80mm l; 9.62–11.36g
Three portions of fork-handles, of
varying lengths, all with terminals in
the form of human torsoes with
rather grotesque faces (see colour
plate)
Girona

9.54 FORK-HANDLES, Silver
39 & 32mm l; 7.07 & 9.99g
Two fork-handles with terminals in
the form of serpents, with enormous
scales the length of their bodies (see
colour plate)
Girona

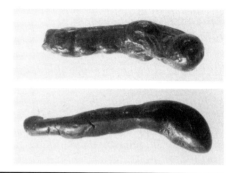

9.55 FORK-HANDLE, Silver
33mm l; 4.55g
Fork-handle with terminal in the
form of a club or possibly a fleur-de-
lys (see colour plate)
Girona

9.56 FORK-HANDLES, Silver
95 & 35mm l; 12.98 & 5.47g
Two fork-handles with terminals in
the form of horses' hooves (see
colour plate)
Girona

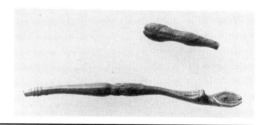

9.57 FORK-PRONGS, Silver
43 & 30mm l; 8.18 & 3.92g
Two five-pronged forks, the tines
parallel and springing from a
shoulder; a small fragment of handle
still in place (see colour plate)
Girona

9.58 FORK-PRONGS, Silver
36 & 46mm l; 9.60 & 15.23g
Two four-pronged forks as above
Girona

9.59 FORK-PRONGS, Silver
44 & 45mm l; 9.88 & 7.38g
Two three-pronged forks (see colour
plate)
Girona

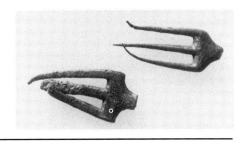

9.60 FORK-PRONG, Silver
36 & 28mm; 4.576 & 3.497g
Fragments of forks with two prongs,
one parallel, the other wish-bone
shaped
Girona

9.61 BOWL, Copper
205mm d
Shallow copper dish with three
original perforations spaced at equal
distances, each 6mm in diameter,
10mm from the rim; decorated on
the outside with a series of parallel
lines above and below the
perforations
Santa Maria de la Rosa

9.62 DISH, Copper
135mm d
Round dish on a short foot and
gently flared base. The bottom has
an opening which is original
La Trinidad Valencera

9.63 CANDLE-STICK, Copper
126mm h
Urn-shaped candle-stick with a
holder 27mm in diameter, sitting in
a saucer-shaped base on a little foot;
damaged
La Trinidad Valencera

9.64 BOWL, Wood

175mm d
Small turned wooden bowl with a
slight shoulder with parallel lines
and a small foot
La Trinidad Valencera

9.65 SPOON, Wood

166mm l
Wooden spoon with large pear-
shaped bowl and short straight
handle decorated with three carved
'X's
La Trinidad Valencera

9.66 KNIFE-HANDLE, Wood and Copper

94mm l
Knife-handle composed of two
tapering pieces of wood held
together with small copper round-
headed rivets; the rivet at the blade-
end is decorated on one side with a
flowery cross, on the other with a
rosette
Girona

9.67 KNIFE-HANDLE, Wood and Copper

88mm l
As above but has been repaired at
one end with a piece of string
Girona

9.68 KNIFE-HANDLE, Wood,
Steel and Cord
140mm l
As above but with a longer section
of cord binding
Girona

9.69 SALT-CELLARS, Wood
56mm d
A pair of salt-cellars in turned wood,
consisting of a small footed bowl on
a flared base; the internal rim is
toothed, apparently to hold a liner
La Trinidad Valencera

9.70 BOWL, Porcelain
152mm d
Small bowl with straight sides on a
little base, in pale blue porcelain,
decorated with darker blue. On the
outside are three classical but lively
horses, between three rather
conventional birds. In the centre of
the interior is a helical ornament.
On the base is the signature of the
maker. Coarse Chinese export
porcelain of the Ming period
La Trinidad Valencera

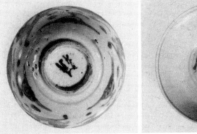

9.71 JUG, Earthenware
155mm h
Rather ovoid handled jug on slight
foot, with pinched top; covered
overall with dark green glaze; several
chips
La Trinidad Valencera

9.72 PLATE, Earthenware
195mm d
Rather coarse earthenware plate,
slightly dished, one half covered
with green glaze, the other half with
blue
La Trinidad Valencera

9.73 PLATE, Earthenware
202mm d
As above but apparently originally
covered with a brown glaze
La Trinidad Valencera

9.74 BOWL, Earthenware
71mm h
Small earthenware bowl with a slight
foot-ring; covered on the inside with
a greeny brown glaze, on the outside
with green; about one quarter is
preserved
La Trinidad Valencera

9.75 SCENT-BOTTLE, Silver
48mm h; 34.82g
Small pear-shaped scent-bottle with
short neck and flat top with an
opening 9mm in diameter; only
about two-thirds survives
Girona

9.76 SCENT-BOTTLE, Silver
28mm h; 24.79g
As above, but less preserved
Girona

9.77 SCENT-BOTTLE, Silver
12mm h; 21.79g
As above, but top only surviving
Girona

9.78 SCENT-BOTTLE, Silver
30mm h; 12.93g
As above, but squashed
Girona

**9.79 SCENT-DROPPER, Crystal
and Silver**
35mm l
Small hexagonal piece of crystal with
ring-handle of silver
Girona

9.80 COMB, Wood
141mm l
Two-sided wooden comb with sawn
teeth, rather coarse on one side, 5
teeth over 10mm, finer on the other,
with 9 teeth every 10mm. Several
teeth are missing on each side. Such
combs were necessary because of the
lice which were endemic on
sixteenth-century ships
La Trinidad Valencera

9.81 TWEEZERS, Bronze
78mm l
A simple strip of bronze 4mm wide
bent back on itself with a loop at the
bend to form a pair of simple
tweezers
Girona

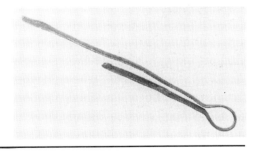

9.82 DRUG-JAR, Earthenware
131mm h
Drug-jar of typical albarello shape
covered inside and out with grey/
white glaze
La Trinidad Valencera

9.83 DRUG-JAR, Earthenware
41mm h
As above but very small
La Trinidad Valencera

9.84 NECK OF STRINGED INSTRUMENT, Wood
355mm l

Length of wood 12mm thick and
45mm wide, with a rounded end
with a central perforation. At the
end where it would have joined to
sounding box of the instrument
there is a slight shoulder on one
side. 18 little grooves have been cut
across and in each is a little insert of
another wood. On the strip nearest
the top it is possible to count up to
26 grooves made by strings
La Trinidad Valencera

9.85 TAMBOURINE, Wood and Copper
35mm h

Several parts, slightly curved, of
which some have rectangular slots,
at approximately 80mm intervals;
each slot is at least 72mm wide. The
cover was attached with little copper
nails. The instrument would have
been about 450mm in diameter
La Trinidad Valencera

9.86 CAGE, Wood
180mm l
Several fragments of a wooden cage,
made rather like a ladder; the largest
portion has 10 little bars and another
still in position at one end covered
by a wooden sleeve-like fitting. The
long portion has transverse holes
presumably for the fitting of the roof
of the cage
La Trinidad Valencera

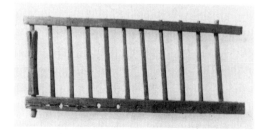

9.87 FISHING-WEIGHTS, Lead
400, 240 & 50g
Three more or less pyramidal pieces
of lead with pointed ends and little
perforations
Girona

9.88 BALL, Wood
58mm d
A small wooden ball, presumably for
some simple ball-game
La Trinidad Valencera

9.89 CHEST OR BOX, Wood
400mm l
Rectangular sheet of wood, 22mm
by 210mm, with tenons and
mortices, and holes for nails or pegs,
at each end. Evidently the end-
piece of a chest or box which may
originally have been covered, e.g.
with leather
La Trinidad Valencera

9.90 ESCUTCHEON, Bronze
57mm l
Rectangular escutcheon of thin sheet
bronze with 8 holes for nails/screws;
'key-hole' shaped opening in middle
Girona

9.91 KEY, Bronze
52mm l
Bronze key, with circular loop
handle and quadrangular barrel
Girona

9.92 KEY, Bronze
37mm l
As above but smaller and with more
complex handle with trefoil form
Girona

9.93 TOP AND STOPPER, Wood
60mm d
Cup-shaped top, of wine-skin which
did not survive conservation-
treatment, with tapering turned
stopper
Girona

9.94 BOX, Wood, iron and silver
100mm w
The remains of two pieces of wood,
both originally regularly hexagonal.
Each is decorated with a central
silver star; in each angle is a little
hole for attachment – in one a little
round-headed nail survives. These
were at one time assumed to be the
two ends of a small concertina;
however since the concertina was not
known before the nineteenth century
they may be assumed to be the top
and bottom of some sort of small
box or container
La Trinidad Valencera

CHAPTER 10
Clothing and Textiles

While a considerable amount of information exists about the clothing of the gentry and nobility in late sixteenth-century Europe, for example from the many portraits that exist of prominent people, considerably less is known about the dress of 'ordinary' folk. When it is remembered that the vast majority of the people on Armada ships were, inevitably, 'ordinary', a serious problem is presented in equating the textiles found with the textiles and clothing worn.

We do know, for instance, that throughout Europe, with allowances for area, climate, station in life and the current mode, male dress, with which inevitably we are mostly concerned, was fairly uniform. It consisted for the most part of a doublet, worn over a shirt, with or without a waistcoat; breeches, reaching to the knees, where they were often tied with ribbon or laces; and below the breeches were worn tight-fitting hose. By and large it would seem that the more fashionable the gentleman, the tighter the breeches and the closer-clinging the hose.

The materials used to make the clothes were much as are now available, excluding, of course, the synthetics. Basics like wool, cotton, silk and linen were available to be used in a variety of ways. We do have some glimmerings of the relative values of different textiles; the register of the cargo of the *Santa Maria de Yciar*, before its fateful and fatal voyage in 1554, showed the differential in tax-payments. For two trunk-loads of silk thread weighing only 143lb (approximately 65kg), a tax of 8 ducats was levied, whereas for five shipments of wool a tax-rate of 1 ducat per 125lb bag (approximately 55kg) was levied. Thus silk was valued at nearly seven times the value of wool. This is not at all surprising, because, as has been said, 'Sheep-breeding meant more to the Iberian economy than the olives, grapes, copper, or even the treasures of Peru'. There were reckoned to be two kinds of sheep in Spain: those with 'ordinary' wool 'who spend their lives in one place, do not change pastures, and return every night to the sheepfold', and the others which 'have fine wool, travel every year, and after spending summer in the mountains go down to the warm meadows of the kingdom'. Notwithstanding this, there were continuing imports of wool from England in the pre-Armada period, particularly of prestigious 'kerseys'.

For the trade in silk from the East it is not necessary to rely totally on historical documents; there are actual objects from wrecks of the late sixteenth century to reinforce the historical evidence. The Venetian merchantship which went down off Gnalic in the Adriatic, as well as carrying guns made in Venice by members of the Alberghetti family which give a link with those from *La Trinidad Valencera*, was also carrying cargo including a roll of silk damask, contained in an iron-bound chest. The roll turned out to be some 54m long and 250mm wide, wrapped in coarse cloth. While the outer layers were badly stained and adhered to the coarse wrapping-material, the inner layers showed the first gleams of the violet gloss of a true damask, both the warp and the weft being of silk of the same purple-violet colour. The decorative effect is achieved by the contrast between the glossy areas carrying the decoration and the matt areas serving as background. The pattern on the roll is a very sophisticated example of Renaissance design and not, indeed, unlike the decoration of some of the silver and silver-gilt fragments from the *Girona*. It consists of cantharus, pomegranate, star and palmette designs, with a repeat every 1,500mm; complete patterns occupy the centre of the field, with halves at the sides, so that the cloth could be joined at the sides to continue the pattern.

This bolt of silk, for which, of course, the raw material was imported from the East, could have been manufactured at any of a number of centres in Europe or in Italy itself, perhaps at Florence, Lucca, Pisa, Bologna, or Venice, though the absence of a Venetian seal on the bale makes this last provenance less likely. It was most probably made in Lucca; but wherever it came from it was a very expensive commodity, more so because it was purple, apparently the most expensive colour of silk.

The wreck at Gnalic contained other textiles, also inside the chest. There were eight black woollen berets, all of the same size, of a type worn by every class and often seen in contemporary portraits, sometimes decorated with a feather. Three white linen shirts were also recovered, all unfortunately in bad condition. Linen appears not to survive prolonged immersion in sea-water very well. Both front and back were made of a single piece of linen, between 660mm and 690mm wide and about 1,140mm long, with slits at the sides at the lower end, rather like modern shirts. Around the neck there is pleating and the shirt is fastened round the neck with a thin plaited cord. The sleeves narrow towards the wrists, which are trimmed with zig-zags. Interestingly, the collars were made of finer linen than the bodies (30 threads per sq cm as opposed to 20), probably as a result of contemporary fashion which caused only the collar to show. Also from the Gnalic wreck came a series of glass beads, basically of white, blue or brown glass, but most frequently multi-coloured, like the bead from *La Trinidad Valencera* (Cat 10.5). Glass beads were not despised in Renaissance Europe; among the jewellery from Schloss Ambras near Innsbruck were several necklaces of glass, probably made by a resident Venetian glass-maker. The beads from the Gnalic wreck were probably made at the famous Murano glassworks in Venice.

The textiles from *La Trinidad Valencera* were not by any means as grand, or complete, as these items from the cargo of a merchantman, preserved in the safety of their original packing. The fragments recovered are either wool or silk and appear to be fragments of garments worn by those on board, presumably stored among their personal possessions and intended as changes of clothing. While some pieces, of wool in particular, are too fragmentary to be identified as being from specific garments, a few can be recognized: a simple pocket-flap (Cat 10.37), of brown wool, with seams along three sides, and two pieces of the yokes of garments, probably doublets (Cat 10.38–10.39), one with gold silk braid along one side, the other with a fine silk cord and each with a poplin finish. Other pieces, including a handsome piece of striped wool, of reddish brown (Cat 9.36), are simply fragments. Recognition of parts of garments is facilitated by the fact that the first manual on tailoring, complete with all its patterns, was published by Juan de Alceya in Madrid in 1589.

While no items of clothing, apart from shoes, appear on the manifests of *La Trinidad Valencera* and while uniforms, in the strict sense, did not exist, there is in the Spanish archives an extant account for 600 complete outfits ordered in 1587. These were for the soldiers serving under Alvaro Flores de Quinones and each outfit consists of a shirt, shoes, underpants, jerkin and hat. The cost of providing such clothing would have been deducted from the wages of the men.

The silk from *La Trinidad Valencera*, while not as magnificent as the roll of damask, is still rather splendid; a gold silk collar, with gold braid surviving along three sides (Cat 10.33), must have belonged to a fairly fashionable gentleman and perhaps would have been part of a garment similar to that to which the gold buttons from the *Girona* (Cat 10.1–10.4) were attached. Two strips of gold braid incorporate their own buttons and button-holes (Cat 10.31–10.32); the two small buttons on one piece, each also covered with gold silk, are probably the reciprocals of the simple loops on the other piece. A single gaiter of poplin-finished silk lined with wool and also with silk-covered buttons (Cat 10.34), was presumably intended to help keep its wearer warm in the cold of the north. The other pieces of silk – ribbons and lengths of delicate cord (Cat 10.28–10.30) – are clearly trimmings and indicate the extravagant style of the sixteenth century, even on board ship. The rather elaborate silk tassel with its intricate netting and fringe (Cat 10.27) is a handsome piece of decoration; Colin Martin has suggested that it may be an example of the kind of tassels sometimes seen hanging from the belts of musketeers of the period.

Some of the textiles had been dyed with cochineal, another commodity imported in vast quantities by the Spanish from the New World. The cargo registered on the *Santa Maria de Yciar* at Veracruz in the months of March and April 1554, just before she sank off Padre Island, includes several consignments of cochineal, packed variously in boxes, barrels and sacks and belonging to several owners. The total carried by this one, not very large ship (about 300 tons), amounted to a staggering 20,654lb (approximately 10,000kg). This is even more impressive when the source of the dye is considered. Cochineal is produced from the bodies of insects of the genus *Dactylopius*, a parasite on two closely related genera of cacti, *Opuntia* and *Nopalea*, both native to Spanish America; the female dies after giving birth, the bodies are collected and then used to make the dye. Since the insect is only a few millimetres in length, the cochineal industry must have been the most labour-intensive in the world.

In addition to the textiles, many pieces of footwear were recovered from *La Trinidad Valencera*. In the manifest are several references to consignments of footwear: one refers to 539 pairs of new leather shoes with two soles, packed in crates of esparto grass; another to 401 pairs of shoes with soles of Spanish leather; and yet another to 2,000 pairs of hempen sandals. Among the shoe-fragments recovered from *La Trinidad Valencera* are not only the soles of such shoes (Cat 10.18–10.26), some of them doubled, as in the manifest entry, but also pieces of uppers (Cat 10.15–10.17). Most shoes at this period were common to both feet; some of those from *La Trinidad Valencera*, however, do appear to differentiate between right and left. For the most part, too, at this period, separate heels were not common, yet some *La Trinidad Valencera* shoes seem to show indications of low, added heels. None of the hempen sandals referred to have been found so far.

Trimmings and fittings for clothing have been recovered from both *La Trinidad Valencera* and the *Girona*. Most of the buckles (Cat 10.12–10.14) recovered from the *Girona* would appear to be too small for belts and may have been used to fasten hose or shoes, although some of the shoes appear to have been fastened with a simple, single lace or ribbon (Cat 10.30). The little rosettes may have been used to decorate helmets. In addition to the textiles from *La Trinidad Valencera* are several items of armour, including helmets or morions of characteristic Spanish shape, and breast-plates. These, unfortunately, while recognisable, are still embedded in concretion and are awaiting conservation.

Sources used for Chapter 10

Braudel, F., *The Mediterranean and the Mediterranean World in the Age of Philip II*, London, 1982
Donkin, R., 'An Ethnogeographical Study of Cochineal and the Opuntia Cactus', *American Philosophical Soc.*, (67) 1977
Flanagan, L., Martin, C., and Stenuit, R., *Tresors de l'Armada*, Brussels, 1985
Martin, C., *Full Fathom Five*, London, 1975
Stenuit, R., *Treasures of the Armada*, London, 1972

Clothing and Textiles

10.1 BUTTONS, Gold
14mm d; 6.44g (average)
A set of eight hollow gold buttons, all slightly deformed; each button has at the top a little attachment loop and, at the bottom, a little knob, like the tail of a gooseberry. Each button is decorated all over in low relief, with, as three central motifs, compositions of quadruple knots (see colour plate)
Girona

10.2 BUTTONS, Gold
14mm d; 3.57g (average)
A set of four hollow gold buttons, all badly deformed, as above. On these the decoration consists of a median series of six circles in low relief, cross-hatched inside with a series of three lines; above and below is a series of six smaller circles containing crosses (see colour plate)
Girona

10.3 BUTTON, Gold
15mm d; 5.04+ g
A single hollow gold button, its
attachment loop missing; the
decoration consists of a central oval
on each of four faces, surrounded by
relief lines and a series of smaller
ovals above and below (see colour
plate)
Girona

10.4 BUTTON, Gold
11mm d; 2.96g
A single hollow gold button, the
decoration consisting of a series of
four median circles with central
lozenges and cross-hatching (see
colour plate)
Girona

10.5 BEAD, Glass
30mm l
A large and rather crude hexagonal
biconical bead of reddish brown
glass, with a central perforation
some 5mm in diameter. The
decoration consists of a median
zig-zag band of blue glass, bordered
with white glass
La Trinidad Valencera

10.6 ROSETTE, Copper
24mm d
An eight-rayed rosette, each petal
decorated with a simple stamped
circle; the central perforation is
4mm in diameter
La Trinidad Valencera

10.7 ROSETTE, Copper
20mm d
As above except that the petals are
plain
La Trinidad Valencera

10.8 ROSETTE, Copper
16mm d
As above but with seven plain petals
La Trinidad Valencera

10.9 ROSETTE, Copper
14mm d
As above but with eight plain petals
La Trinidad Valencera

10.10 ROSETTE, Copper
11mm d
A little domed copper rosette, like a
little shell with 12 radial ridges and
no central perforation. There is a
small trace of solder on the back
La Trinidad Valencera

10.11 ROSETTE, Gold
14mm d; 0.97g
As above
Girona

10.12 BUCKLE, Copper
55mm w
Large copper buckle, the guard
bow-shaped, the bar for the
attachment of the belt 31mm across;
the tongue is a simple flat elongated
triangle
Girona

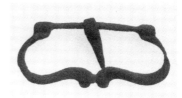

10.13 BUCKLE, Copper
25mm w
A simple D-shaped copper buckle,
the bar for the strap 14mm across;
the tongue is straight and pointed
Girona

10.14 BUCKLE, Copper
23mm w
A small simple rectangular buckle,
with a strap-bar 13mm across; the
tongue is missing
Girona

10.15 SHOE-UPPER, Leather
150mm l
The two side-pieces of the heel-end
of a shoe upper in brown leather,
the grain-side out, no longer
attached along the back seam; at the
front are two perforated tongues,
45mm long; a length of reddish
brown ribbon is still in place in one
of the holes
La Trinidad Valencera

10.16 SHOE-UPPER, Leather
110mm w
The two side-pieces of the heel-end
of a shoe-upper, still held together
by a strip of leather even though the
stitching has disappeared; of nice
black leather
La Trinidad Valencera

10.17 SHOE-UPPER, Leather
182mm l
The front portion of a shoe-upper of
black leather, with a rounded toe;
complete as far as the side-seam.
The stitching holes for attachment to
the sole and the back are still there
La Trinidad Valencera

10.18 SHOE-SOLE, Leather
230mm l
Simple sole of brown leather,
suitable for either left or right foot;
20mm wide in the middle. The heel-
end is squared. Traces of stitching
survive where the upper was
attached
La Trinidad Valencera

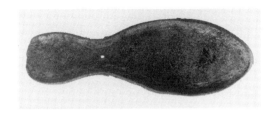

10.19 SHOE-SOLE, Leather
232mm l
As above but narrower (22mm) and
with a gently pointed toe
La Trinidad Valencera

10.20 SHOE-SOLE, Leather
215mm+ l
Double leather sole, the toe-end
missing; wide-fitting (43mm); black
leather
La Trinidad Valencera

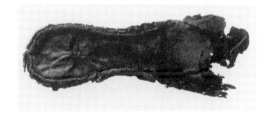

10.21 SHOE-SOLE, Leather
218mm l
As above but apparently from a left
shoe; quite narrow-fitting (22mm);
toe-end rather squared
La Trinidad Valencera

10.22 SHOE-SOLE, Leather
224mm l
Sole of black leather, slightly curved
and apparently belonging to a left
shoe; narrow-fitting (19mm) and
toe-end gently rounded
La Trinidad Valencera

10.23 SHOE-SOLE, Leather
246mm l
Double sole of brown leather; the
underside is worn in places. Quite
wide-fitting (35mm); the toe is broad
and round; traces of very regular
stitching survive
La Trinidad Valencera

10.24 SHOE-SOLE, Leather
209mm l
Double sole of black leather;
narrow-fitting (18mm) with rounded
toe
La Trinidad Valencera

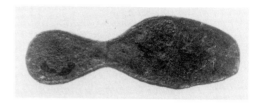

10.25 SHOE-SOLE, Leather
235mm l
Double sole of black leather, with
rounded toe; the upper layer is cut
across just at the heel
La Trinidad Valencera

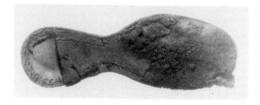

10.26 SHOE-SOLE, Leather
160mm+ l
Portion of a sole adaptable for either
foot, slightly curved
La Trinidad Valencera

10.27 TASSEL, Silk
180mm l
Gold silk tassel, ending in a knot;
from this is suspended a net
composed of lozenges, about 5mm x
5mm, knotted at the corners. The
lower end is decorated with a fringe
La Trinidad Valencera

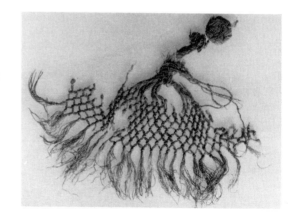

10.28 CORD, Silk
75mm w
Bundle of very fine gold silk cord, of
Z2S composition
La Trinidad Valencera

10.29 CORD, Silk
110mm w
Bundle of red silk cord, of Z2S
composition,with little knots at the
ends; dyed with cochineal
La Trinidad Valencera

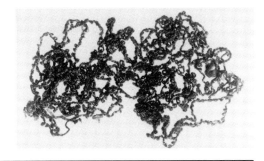

10.30 RIBBON, Silk
120mm w
Length of pink taffeta-weave silk,
dyed with cochineal
La Trinidad Valencera

10.31 BRAID, Silk
9mm w
Length of gold silk braid, the end of
which has four loops for buttons and
embroidered decoration
La Trinidad Valencera

10.32 BRAID, Silk
9mm w
Length of gold silk braid, the end of
which bears two silk-covered
buttons; probably the reciprocal of
the above
La Trinidad Valencera

**10.33 COLLAR, Silk, Wool and
Jute**
500mm l
Narrow collar of gold silk velvet
with gold silk braid surviving along
three sides and part of the fourth;
there is a woollen lining and part of
an interlining of jute
La Trinidad Valencera

10.34 GAITER, Silk and Wool
190mm w
Gaiter of brown silk, with poplin
finish, in the form of an inverted
crown; there are traces of woollen
lining; two buttons covered with silk
and two button-holes survive
La Trinidad Valencera

10.35 FRAGMENT, Wool
73mm w
Fragment of reddish brown wool
La Trinidad Valencera

10.36 FRAGMENT, Wool
290mm w
Fragment of striped wool of reddish
brown, with darker parallel stripes,
one 25mm wide, the other 40mm
La Trinidad Valencera

10.37 POCKET-FLAP, Wool
255mm l
Piece of curved quadrangular wool
with seams on three sides
La Trinidad Valencera

10.38 YOKE, Wool and Silk
295mm w
Yoke of a garment in finely woven
brown wool with a poplin finish.
Gold silk braid along one side
La Trinidad Valencera

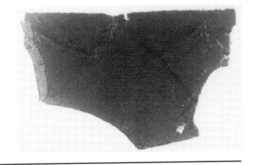

10.39 YOKE, Wool and Silk
280mm l
As above, but with a fine silk cord
La Trinidad Valencera

10.40 SOCK, Wool
440mm l
A sock in brown woollen serge, with
a double seam along the sides
La Trinidad Valencera

CHAPTER 11
Money

The understanding of sixteenth-century history, involving political, religious, commercial and other considerations, is complex and difficult. Perhaps one of the factors that makes it so is the use, in the Armada context, of the term 'Spain' in reference to the protagonist on one side. Although by 1588 the Iberian peninsula was, in fact, 'Spanish', this had not been so for very long, any more than by the same period Italy was 'Italian'.

It was as late as 1479 that the 'Spanish' kingdoms of Aragon and Castile were united, as a result of the marriage of Ferdinand of Aragon and Isabella of Castile, which marked the start of the fusing together of previously independent states.

One of the couples' first distinctions was their being granted by the Pope in 1492 the right to call themselves 'the Catholic Kings', in recognition of the fact that in that year the final Moorish stronghold, Granada, was at long last conquered; in addition some 170,000 Jews, who declined the offer of baptism, were expelled from the country. The acquisition of the Kingdom of Naples made Spain a serious challenger of France's position as the most powerful state in Europe. Royal arranged marriages were a common political and diplomatic device of the period and Ferdinand made good use of his crop of daughters: Catherine was betrothed first to Arthur of England and then, on his death, to Henry, his brother; Joana was married to Philip, the Hapsburg prince who ruled the Burgundian Netherlands; Isabella to Alfonso of Portugal; and Maria to Manuel, who succeeded to the throne of Portugal after Alfonso's death a few months after his marriage. A great web of marital connections throughout Europe was spun, which was to have far-reaching consequences.

One immediate consequence of these marriages was that, on the death in 1504 of Isabella, her daughter Joana and the Hapsburg prince Philip, ruled briefly in Castile, while Ferdinand was forced to take a back seat for two years until Philip's death in 1506. At this time, his daughter Joana being unfit to rule because of mental illness, he became undisputed ruler again. Charles, the son of Philip and Joana, who, as Charles V, was to accede to the rule of the Holy Roman Empire in 1519, had been reared in the Netherlands and could not even speak Spanish. He succeeded his grandfather on the Spanish throne in 1517, as Charles I of Spain, ruling jointly, at first, with his mad mother. He failed to achieve great popularity in Spain, and his succession to his grandfather's title of Holy Roman Emperor seems to have been secured by bribery. His success in gaining this honour totally alienated Francois I of France who had also entertained hopes of the Emperorship and was one contributory cause of a series of wars with France.

Meanwhile, of the other strategic marriages arranged by Ferdinand and Isabella, some prospered, others did not: Catherine of Aragon was divorced by Henry VIII when he decided that he wished to marry Anne Boleyn, in order to acquire a legitimate male heir instead of Mary, the sole offspring he and Catherine had produced. John, son of Maria and Manuel of Portugal, succeeded to the throne of Portugal in 1521 as the third king of that name and his sister became the wife of the Emperor Charles V, King Charles I of Spain, her first cousin.

It was against this 'Spanish' background in 1492, that backed by Isabella of Castile, a Genoese seaman, Cristoforo Colombo, made the first of four voyages and discovered the 'New World'; in doing so he shaped European history in the sixteenth century and subsequently world history. Despite rather a shakey start – the greed of many of his companions had caused a considerable amount of dissension among the first to colonise the new discoveries – this New World was to finance Spain's many campaigns throughout the sixteenth century and, ultimately, to make the Armada of 1588 a financial possibility and then a reality.

The native jewellery and the enormous gold nuggets brought back by the Columban voyages had shown that there was likely to be enormous wealth available in the new lands; the exploitation of that wealth was to tax the ingenuity of Europe to the full. Although Columbo himself had succeeded in going to America and getting back four times, it was no easy undertaking, as many of his successors were to find to their cost. Even Magellan, the instigator of the first successful circumnavigation of the world, begun in 1519 and lasting for slightly over three years, died on the return leg of the journey – not because of any inadequacies as a seaman, but because of the treachery of a native ruler in the Philippines.

The *Casa de Contratacion* was established in 1503, its purpose to encourage and control trade with the Indies; its headquarters were located in Seville, the major city in Castile. (This gave the lie to the concept of total unity, as trade with the Indies was considered virtually a Castilian monopoly.) As well as establishing a hydrographic bureau and school of navigation as early as 1508 and regulating the size, maintenance and manning of the vessels involved in the trade with the Indies, the *Casa* was closely involved with maintaining close records and close control of the trade itself. Since the trade with the Indies was to become, increasingly, the major source of royal wealth, so the *Casa* was to have greater powers to control and tax and protect it. A series of ordinances was issued laying down regulations and penalties for their violation, all of which were brought together in 1552.

This, inevitably, led to the establishment of a great bureaucracy. A clerk, appointed by the *Casa*, had to accompany each ship, to list every item of cargo and the manner of its stowing, to ensure that all taxes were duly paid and to combat any attempts at smuggling. An inspector of the *Casa* had to inspect the condition of the ship, its rigging and its ordnance; until he was satisfied, the vessel could not sail.

One of the taxes to be collected was the *averia*, to pay the cost of protecting from pirates ships engaged in the Indies trade. To begin with this operated only in the approaches to Spanish ports, but later, from 1537, for the course of the whole journey. The vessels used for this escort duty were the forerunners of the galleons of the Indian Guard which served in the Squadron of Castile of the Armada of 1588.

It is interesting that there is tangible evidence of an attempt to evade the attentions of the *Casa* and, despite the severe penalties, to attempt to smuggle silver. While the wreck in question is that of the *Nuestra Senora de la Pura y Limpia Concepcion*, wrecked in 1641, there can be little doubt that similar attempts had been frequent. Among the material salvaged from *La Concepcion* were the remains of a chest with a false bottom concealing 1,440 silver pieces of eight.

While figures do not exist for the total imports of gold and silver from the New World, some startling figures are preserved. For New Spain, from 1522 to 1557, the Crown's share of exports of precious metals amounted to slightly more than 2,750,000 pesos; for the period from 1558 to 1601 it exceeded 34,385,000 pesos. Just for Potosi, in Bolivia, where a complete hill of silver had been found in 1570, the receipts varied between 133,885 pesos in 1572 to 982,979 in 1593. A new extraction process, using mercury, which had been introduced in 1554, increased production at the mines; the process previously in use had been so inefficient that ores producing less than 1/160 of silver could not be used.

At the mines, after smelting, the silver extracted from the ore was shaped into planchas, the Crown tax levied and the discs of silver stamped. Such stamped silver planchas were among the items recovered from the Padre Island wrecks, showing that tax had been paid and indicating the mine from which the bullion had originated. Some of the silver was struck into coin in the colonies; mints existed at Mexico, Lima and Potosi, where, indeed, the ruins of the sixteenth-century mint still stand. Examples of silver coins struck at these mints are among the coins from the *Girona*.

One of the great difficulties in sixteenth-century Europe with regard to trade and commerce, and even with regard to understanding sheer quantities of materials, is the lack of any kind of standardisation of weights and measures or, indeed, of coinage. Among the dry goods embarked on *La Trinidad Valencera*, according to the manifest, some are weighed 'peso de Castilla', others 'peso de Sicilia' and the extra anchor embarked is weighed in 'peso de San Sebastian'. The *Girona*, when she left Naples, was carrying 200 quintals of gunpowder, in Neapolitan pounds; at Lisbon she embarked a further 208 quintals in Castilian pounds. Not only was there a separate unit of weight for different provinces or even towns, but also the values could vary by almost any factor. The Neapolitan pound is reckoned to be the equivalent of 891g, the Castilian pound of 460g (as compared to the *avoirdupois* pound at 453.6g); other Iberian pounds varied from 575g, for Coruna, to a miserly 345g for Avila. This is why it was necessary for those listing the loading of supplies to record carefully what measure was being used. The same variation is to be seen among liquid measures, where some wine for *La Trinidad Valencera* was measured 'medida de Portugal', other wine was measured 'medida de Castilla' and the oil in 'medida de Seville'. The Castilian arroba, as we saw with reference to *La Trinidad Valencera*'s olive jars, equates to 12.56l.

With the values of coins, similar problems are encountered. The only easy exchange rates are those between similarly named coins, of the same metal; a one escudo gold piece really is worth half the value of a two escudo gold piece and the weights to a certain extent support this: a one escudo gold piece weighs about 3.306g; a two escudo piece about 6.683g. The discrepancy is accounted for by the differential rate of taxation and the fact that essentially it costs as much to produce a small coin as a large one.

It is against this sort of background that the coins recovered from Armada wrecks, predominantly the *Girona*, must be considered. The 1,320 coins from the *Girona*, 414 of gold, 789 in silver and 122 in base metal, constitute a very large and important hoard, about the circumstances of whose deposition there can be no argument. A simple analysis of the collection shows that, as might be expected, over 78 per cent of the coins derive from the Spanish mainland. Of the gold coins from this source almost 85 per cent were struck at Seville, the mint nearest to Lisbon where the Armada gathered; again, of the silver, over 53 per cent comes from this mint. Despite the fact that the coinage from the *Girona* was all 'private' – the personal wealth of those on board – much of it will, nonetheless, have come from official sources, for example, in the form of pay. To this basic component must be added, however, the coinage acquired by those on board from other sources: change received on shore, money in their possession before joining the fleet, etc. Since there were survivors from at least two other ships on board the *Girona*, the variety among this material is not surprising. All in all there are coins from fourteen different mints in six different countries: from the Spanish mainland, in addition to

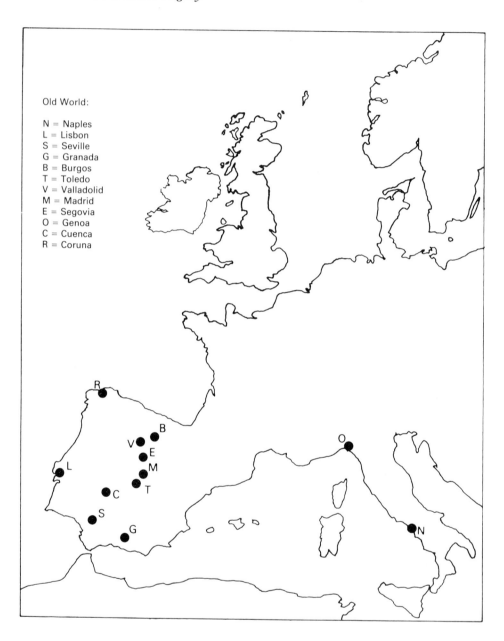

Old World:

N = Naples
L = Lisbon
S = Seville
G = Granada
B = Burgos
T = Toledo
V = Valladolid
M = Madrid
E = Segovia
O = Genoa
C = Cuenca
R = Coruna

Locations of mints where the *Girona* coins were struck

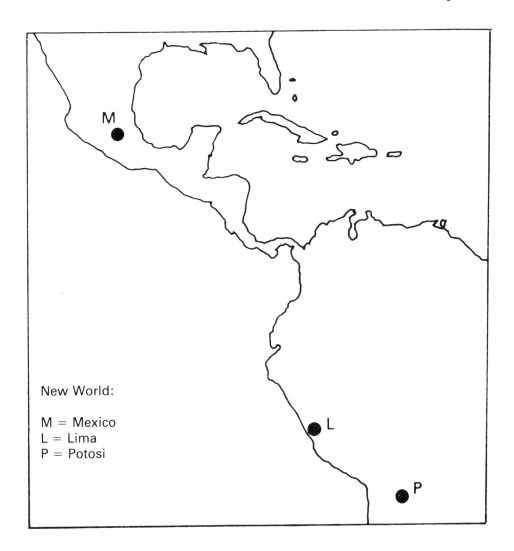

New World:

M = Mexico
L = Lima
P = Potosi

those from Seville there are coins from Toledo, Segovia, Madrid, Burgos, Cuenca, Granada, Valladolid and Coruna; from the Americas, from the mints at Mexico, Lima and Potosi; and, inevitably, since the *Girona* herself came from Naples, from the mint there, which in fact produced by far the most handsome coins in the collection, bearing fine portrait busts.

The gold coins predictably survived their immersion in seawater for close on 400 years much better than the silver ones; the inscriptions are much easier to read, the details of the decoration are much clearer. In their turn; the silver coins are in much better condition than those of copper, many of which are little more than flat discs, on which the inscriptions can scarcely be read; as might be expected these lower denomination coins tend to be from Naples and Portugal.

Sources used for chapter 11

Arnold, J.B., and Weddle, R.S., *The Nautical Archeology of Padre Island*, London, 1978

Castan, C. and Cayan, J.R., *Las Monedas Espagnoles*, Madrid, 1978

Flanagan, L., 'Steelyards and Steelyard Weights', *International J. Nautical Archaeol*, (16) 1987

Flanagan, L., Martin, C. and Stenuit, R., *Tresors de l'Armada*, Brussels, 1985

Martin, C., *Full Fathom Five*, London, 1975

Oliva, J. de Y., *Catalogo de los Reales de a Ocho Espanoles*, Madrid, 1965

Peterson, M., *Treasures of the Concepcion*, Chicago, 1980

Stenuit, R., *Treasures of the Armada*, London, 1972

Money

11.1 EIGHT-REAL PIECE, Silver
38mm d; 21.373g
Round silver eight-real piece of
Philip II, with Arms of Spain on
obverse, with P & B on left-hand
side, star and D on right; Arms of
Castile on reverse. Lima mint,
assayer Diego de la Torre.
Inscription on obverse reads:
*PHILIPPVS D G
HISPANIARVM B T*; on reverse:
INDIARVM REX. This and the

12.5 Agnus Dei Reliquary, gold, from the *Girona*. The hinged lid is decorated in relief, with a central area framed by pillars and topped with a pediment containing a representation of St John the Baptist. The interior is divided into five circular compartments, with a central raised portion corresponding to a receptacle accessed from the back, presumably originally containing a relic over which a cover, held in place by the same sort of architectural frame as appears on the front, fitted

13.25 Necklace or Collar, gold with lapis lazuli and pearl. One of a presumed set of twelve mounts for portrait-cameos of Roman Emperors, from the *Girona*. The lapis lazuli portrait is almost in its original condition and still bears its original complement of eight pearls, held on a fine gold wire. At the top is a little grotesque mask; the shoulders supporting this have a little setting filled with green enamel

next seven coins are representative
of the immense wealth in gold, as
well as silver, from the New World
Philip II (1556–1598)
Girona

11.2 EIGHT-REAL PIECE, Silver
40mm d; 24.995g
As above
Girona

11.3 EIGHT-REAL PIECE, Silver
39mm d; 24.995g
As above
Girona

11.4 EIGHT-REAL PIECE, Silver
40mm d; 25.088g
As above
Girona

11.5 EIGHT-REAL PIECE, Silver
39mm d; 21.855g
As above
Girona

11.6 EIGHT-REAL PIECE, Silver
42mm d; 21.532g
As above but Mexico mint (M with
circle)
Girona

11.7 EIGHT-REAL PIECE, Silver
38mm d; 24.835g
As above
Girona

11.8 FOUR-REAL PIECE, Silver
31mm d; 8.868g
Rather badly eroded; legible
inscription on obverse: 'PHI'; on
reverse *REX HISPANIARVM
ET . .* ; Mexico mint
Girona

11.9 FOUR ESCUDOS, Gold
30mm d; 13.363g
Round gold four escudo piece, a
little clipped; Arms of Spain on
obverse, of Castile on reverse;
inscription on obverse:
PHILIPPVS II DEI GRATIA, on
reverse *HISPANIARVM REX.*
Seville mint (S), the mint most
widely represented among the gold
coins from the *Girona*, amounting to
almost 85 per cent of them
Girona

11.10 FOUR ESCUDOS, Gold
30mm d; 13.399g
As above
Girona

11.11 FOUR ESCUDOS, Gold
32mm d; 13.427g
As above
Girona

11.12 FOUR ESCUDOS, Gold
29mm d; 13.498g
As above
Girona

11.13 FOUR ESCUDOS, Gold
30mm d; 13.410g
As above
Girona

11.14 FOUR ESCUDOS, Gold
29mm d; 13.531g
As above but bent
Girona

11.15 TWO ESCUDOS, Gold
25mm d; 6.727g
Round gold coin with Arms of Spain
on obverse, of Castile on reverse;
obverse inscription reads:
PHILIPPVS II DEI GRATIA,
reverse *HISPANIARVM REX*
Seville mint
Girona

11.16 TWO ESCUDOS, Gold
27mm d; 6.690g
As above
Girona

11.17 TWO ESCUDOS, Gold
25mm d; 6.668g
As above
Girona

11.18 TWO ESCUDOS, Gold
25mm d; 6.765g
As above, but Toledo mint
Girona

11.19 TWO ESCUDOS, Gold
25mm d; 6.713g
As above
Girona

11.20 TWO ESCUDOS, Gold
27mm d; 6.698g
As above, but Segovia mint
Girona

11.21 ESCUDO, Gold
21mm d; 3.303g
Small round gold coin with Arms of
Spain on obverse, of Castile on
reverse; obverse inscription reads:
IOANA ET CAROLVS D, reverse:
*HISPANIARVM REGES
SICILIE*; Seville mint. Joan and
Charles I (1506–1516)
Girona

11.22 ESCUDO, Gold
22mm d; 3.335g
As above
Girona

11.23 ESCUDO, Gold
24mm d; 3.314g
As above
Girona

11.24 ESCUDO, Gold
23mm d; 3.317g
Small round gold coin, with on
obverse laureate head to right; on
reverse Arms of Spain. Obverse
inscription: *CAROLUS V
ROMANO IMPERAT*, reverse: *R.
ARAGO V SI*. Naples mint. Charles
I of Spain as Charles V of Holy
Roman Empire.
This and the following coins
demonstrate the superior artistic
quality of the coinage minted in
Sicily with the fine Renaissance
portraits
Girona

11.25 ESCUDO, Gold
22mm d; 3.324g
As above but obverse inscription
reads: *CAROLVS IIIII ROM IMP*
and reverse: *R. ARAG VTRIVS*
Girona

11.26 ESCUDO, Gold
23mm d; 3.342g
As above but obverse inscription
reads: *CAROLVS IIIII ROM IMP*
Girona

11.27 SCUDO D'ORO, Gold
23mm d; 3.296g
Small round gold coin, with obverse
laureate head to right; reverse Arms
of Spain; obverse inscription reads:
PHILIPP D G REX ARA VTRI S
1582, reverse: *SICILIAE*
HIERVSA. Naples mint
Girona

11.28 SCUDO D'ORO, Gold
24mm d; 3.293g
As above but obverse reads
PHILIPP REX ARA VTRI 1582
Girona

11.29 SCUDO D'ORO, Gold
24mm d; 3.373g
As above
Girona

11.30 SCUDO D'ORO, Gold
24mm d; 3.365g
As above
Girona

11.31 SCUDO D'ORO, Gold
23mm d; 3.375g
Early type with on obverse Arms as
Holy Roman Emperor, on double-
headed eagle; on reverse floreated
Cross. Obverse inscription:
CAROLVS V RO IM, reverse
HISPAN VTRIVS SICIL R R.
Naples mint
Girona

11.32 SCUDO D'ORO, Gold
24mm d; 3.349g
As above but obverse inscription
reads: *CAROLVS V RO IMP* and
reverse: *HISPARVM VTRIVS
SICI R R*
Girona

11.33 SCUDO D'ORO, Gold
23mm d; 3.363g
Later type with on obverse laureate
head to right; reverse with
Emperor's Arms on double-headed
eagle; obverse inscription:
CAROLVS IIIII ROM IM,
reverse: *R ARAG VTRIVS.*
Girona

11.34 SCUDO D'ORO, Gold
23mm d; 3.300g
As above except that obverse has
final 'P' to 'IM'
Girona

11.35 EIGHT REAL-PIECE, Silver
3.7mm d; 16.986g
Round silver coin, not very well
preserved; on obverse Arms of
Spain, on reverse those of Castile.
Inscriptions not well preserved: that
on obverse clearly contains:
PHILIPP; that on reverse illegible.
Toledo mint
Girona

11.36 EIGHT-REAL PIECE, Silver
36mm d; 24.692g
As above, but better preserved.
Seville mint
Girona

11.37 EIGHT-REAL PIECE, Silver
37mm d; 27.328g
As above but better preserved:
obverse inscription reads:
PHILIPPVS II, reverse: *REX HI*
Girona

11.38 EIGHT-REAL PIECE, Silver
39mm d; 21.324g
As above but clearer inscriptions:
obverse: *PHILIPPVS D G*
HISPANIARVM, reverse:
INDIARVM REX
Girona

11.39 EIGHT-REAL PIECE, Silver
42mm d; 23.481g
Obverse crowned Arms of Castile
and Leon quartering Aragon and
Sicily; reverse Yoke and Arrows;
Obverse inscription reads:
FERNANDVS ELIZABET,
reverse: *REX ET REGINA*
CASTILE LEGIONIS. Issued by
Charles I in the name of his
grandparents Ferdinand and Isabel.
Seville mint
Girona

11.40 FOUR-REAL PIECE, Silver
33mm d; 9.008g
As above, but smaller; inscription
illegible except for 'G'; Granada
mint; *PHILIP II*
Girona

11.41 FOUR-REAL PIECE, Silver
32mm d; 10.033g
As above
Girona

11.42 ESCUDO, Silver
37mm d; 42.924g
Larger round silver coin with
bearded head to right on obverse
and inscription (not totally legible):
PHILIP R AN NEAP PR HISP;
on reverse inscription: *HILARITAS
UNIVERSA*. Naples mint
Girona

11.43 ESCUDO, Silver
40mm d; 20.812g
As above – slightly less well
preserved
Girona

11.44 ESCUDO, Silver
35mm d; 19.670g
As above, but more abraded
Girona

11.45 FIVE-TARI PIECE, Silver
35mm d; 10.523g
Round silver coin, armoured bust to
right on obverse, with inscription:
PHILIPP REX ARAGON VT; on
reverse Arms of Spain and
inscription: *SICIL ET
HIERUSAL*. Naples mint
Girona

11.46 FIVE-TARI PIECE, Silver
35mm d; 11.564g
As above
Girona

11.47 FIVE-TARI PIECE, Silver
34mm d; 12.560g
As above
Girona

11.48 FIVE-TARI PIECE, Silver
33mm d; 11.882g
As above but obverse inscription
reads: *PHILIPP D G REX ARA V*
Girona

11.49 TESTONE, Silver
27mm d; 4.026g
Small silver coin, obverse bare-
headed bust in armour and
inscription: *PHILIP R ANG B
PRI HI*, reverse: *POPVLOR
SECVRITATI*, Philip as King of
England, 1554–6. Naples mint
Girona

11.50 TESTONE, Silver
28mm d; 3.679g
As above
Girona

11.51 TWO-TARI PIECE, Silver
27mm d; 3.934g
Small round coin, obverse with bare-
headed bust in armour and
inscription: *PHILIPP R ARAGN
VT*, reverse Arms of Spain and
inscription: *SICIL ET HIERVSA.*
Naples mint
Girona

11.52 TWO-TARI PIECE, Silver
25mm d; 3.993g
As above
Girona

CHAPTER 12
Religion

The religious composition of sixteenth-century Europe was not totally dissimilar to that of twentieth-century Europe, at least in respect of those areas which were predominantly Protestant or Roman Catholic: England, the Dutch part of the Low Countries and Germany were all Protestant; Italy, Spain and, with the exception of the Huguenot element, France were Roman Catholic. Scotland, an independent kingdom still, at this time had a large and powerful Roman Catholic element; Ireland, with the Plantations still in the future and the only English being those present in an official capacity, was overwhelmingly Roman Catholic.

The religious element in the Armada must not be underestimated. Philip obviously regarded the invasion as being in the service of God and the English quite unequivocally regarded it as a threat as much to their religious liberty as to their civil liberty. The propagandists in England were not slow to kindle the religious spark into a flame. Rumours were spread, as a contemporary foreign correspondent in London said:

> Being in great alarm, they made the people believe that the Spaniards were bringing a shipload of halters in the Armada to hang all the Englishmen, and another shipload of scourges to whip women, with 3,000 or 4,000 wet nurses to suckle the infants. It was said that all children between the ages of 7 and 12 would be branded in the face so that they might always be known.

Perhaps their recent experience at the hands of Mary, Philip's wife, made it easier for the English to believe this sort of misinformation. Mary's attempts to achieve reunion with Rome were reversed under Elizabeth; the Act of Supremacy of 1559 abolished Papal power and the Act of Uniformity made the Book of Common Prayer the only legal form of worship. Elizabeth herself, of course, had been excommunicated by the Pope. Foxe's *Book of Martyrs* immortalised not only the martyrs, but the fires in which they had been burned and served to generate an enduring hatred and fear of Rome.

The situation in Ireland was interesting. On the accession of Queen Mary there had been jubilation, as an account written by the staunchly Protestant Bishop of Ossory, of the rejoicings in Kilkenny, shows:

On the twentieth day of August was the Lady Mary with us at Kilkenny proclaimed Queen of England, France and Ireland, with the greatest solemnity that there could be devised, of processions, musters and disguisings; all the noble captains and gentlemen thereabouts being present. What-a-do I had that day with the prebendaries and priests about wearing the cope, crozier and mitre in procession, it were too much to write . . . On the Thursday, which was the last day of August, I being absent, the clergy of Kilkenny, by procurement of that wicked justice Hothe, blasphemously resumed again the whole Papism, or heap of superstitions of the Bishop of Rome; to the utter contempt of Christ and His Holy Word, of the King and Council of England, and of all ecclesiastical and politic order, without either statute or yet proclamation. They rung all the bells in the cathedral, minster and parish churches: they flung up their caps to the battlement of the great temple, with smilings and laughings most dissolutely . . . they brought forth their copes, candle sticks, holy water stock, cross and censers; they mustered forth in general procession most gorgeously, all the town over, with '*Sancta Maria*', '*ora pro nobis*' and the rest of the Latin litany: they chattered it, they chanted it, with great noise and devotion: they banqueted all the day after, for that they were delivered from the grace of God into a warm sun.

A letter from Archbishop Loftus of Dublin to Lord Burghley goes a long way to showing the Irish attitude both to the Armada and its defeat and to the official, Protestant, forms of worship:

I assure your Lordship their obstinacy now is such that unless they be enforced, they will not ever come to hear the Word preached, as by experience we observed at the time appointed by the Lord Deputy and Council for a general assembly of all the noblemen and gentlemen of every county, after Her Majesty's good success against the Spaniard, to give God thanks for the same. At which time, notwithstanding the Sheriff of every county did their duties with all diligence, and warned all men to repair to the principal church in every county, wherein order was taken for public prayers and thanksgivings unto God, together with a sermon to be preached by choice men in every diocese, yet very few or none almost resorted thereunto, but even in Dublin itself the lawyers, in term time, took occasion to leave the town of purpose to absent themselves from that godly exercise – so betraying in themselves, besides their corruption in religion, great want of duty and loyalty unto her Majesty.

Philip, of course, took his religion very seriously indeed. His grand palace at El Escorial, with its 4,000 rooms, 88 staircases and 100 miles of corridors, was as monastic as it was palatial and wore the dome of its basilica like a crown. Here, in a small windowless room like a sparsely furnished monk's cell, Philip interrupted his work with periodic prayer-sessions in the private chapel next door and from here he emphasised the religious, missionary and crusading aspects of the Armada. It was from the King himself that the moral instructions issued by the Duke of Medina Sidonia originated. Philip wrote to the Duke:

Since victories are in the hands of God, to give and to take away as He sees fit, and since your cause is so peculiarly His as to assure you of His help and favour, if this is not undeserved by sinfulness, great care must be taken that none is committed in this fleet, and in particular that no blasphemy is uttered, under pain of the most severe punishment to be carried out publicly, in order that the chastisement for having tolerated such blasphemy may not descend upon all.

The Duke issued instructions to the fleet:

First and foremost, it must be clearly understood by all, from the highest to the lowest, that the principal aim of His Majesty is the service of God. No one, therefore, must sail without confessing and communicating in true repentance for his sins. Similarly, to utter any oath or to take in vain the name of Our Lord, or of Our Lady or of the Saints is forbidden on pain of the most severe punishments and stoppages of wine. Gambling is prohibited, forbidden games in particular and especially at night. It is well known what inconvenience and offence to God is caused by the presence of public or private women. I therefore forbid that any be taken on board.

There were constant reminders of the Holy purpose: the sails bore the Holy Cross in red; before the Armada sailed from Lisbon, the sacred banner of the crusade, with its inscription (in Latin) 'Arise, O Lord, and vindicate Thy Cause', was taken from the high altar of the Cathedral; every morning the ships' boys said matins and every evening vespers; *'Ave Maria'*, *'Salve Regina'* and the litany were rotated; there were some 180 priests and monks among the nearly 30,000 on board the 130 ships; the days of the week were renamed: Sunday was 'Jesus', Monday 'Holy Ghost', Tuesday 'Most Holy Trinity', Wednesday 'Santiago', Thursday 'The Angels', Friday 'All Saints' and Saturday 'Our Lady'.

Even the names of the ships in the Armada constituted an ever-present reminder; of the original 130 ships in the force a full 96 bore names of saints. Four were called *San Juan*; two more *San Juan Bautista* and a further three *San Juan* in combination with a qualifying term; six were *Santiagos* and five were *Trinidads*. By contrast in the English fleet not a saint's name is to be found; the nearest approach is possibly the *Ascension* or the more Protestant-sounding *Gift of God*. For the most part, however, names such as *Triumph*, *White Bear* or *Tyger* were preferred.

When the English coast was eventually sighted, the banner that was hoisted bore the image of Christ Crucified with the Virgin on one side of Him and Mary Magdalen on the other. Three shots were fired 'as a signal to every man to make his prayer'.

Not merely the *San Martin*, the flagship of Medina Sidonia, boasted a religious banner; the painted linen banner taken from the *San Mateo* when she ran aground on the Flemish sandbanks and now preserved in Leiden portrays the Crucifixion, which makes it likely that, at least, all the major ships carried such banners. Religious medals had been distributed wholesale among the men; examples have been recovered from all the Irish wrecks, many of them bearing the head of Christ, some the Madonna and Child, some the Crucifixion (Cat 12.6–12.13). (Surprisingly, perhaps, none seem to have been observed on *El Gran Grifon*.)

The other symbolic items from the wrecks do little more than remind us of the emphasis placed on the religious aspects of the Armada by Philip II. It is, perhaps, appropriate that things spiritual should not be excessively represented in material form. The three crucifixes that have survived (Cat 12.1–12.3), all from the *Girona*, may have been worn, or used, by some of the 180 clerics of the Armada, some of whom may have been among the 1,300 crowded onto this ship when she sank. The ring inscribed 'IHS' (not a signet ring in the strict sense since the letters are not a mirror image) may have belonged to a member of the Society of Jesus. Certainly Jesuits had been active in Ireland; one Charles MacMorris, who was also skilled in medicine and chirurgery, had tended the Roman Catholic Archbishop of Cashel while he was in prison in Dublin, after he had been tortured and before he was put to death in 1584. Some may even have been among the Irish clerics who accompanied the Armada. At least two are known: the Bishop of Killaloe, who is said to have perished on the *Girona*, and one Tomas Vitres, described as '*clergio Irlandes*'.

The gold *Agnus Dei* reliquary (Cat 12.5) in the form of a book is probably the grandest religious item from the *Girona*. It has been suggested that it may actually have been in the possession of the Bishop of Killaloe. It is, perhaps, surprising that St John is not carrying the Lamb of God, as he so often does. It would have been particularly appropriate on a container designed to hold the little pellets of wax, made from Paschal candles, blessed by the Pope and imbued with great protective properties. Sometimes the *Agnus Dei*, instead of having the form of small pellets of wax, like those found on the *Girona*, were stamped or cast rather like the religious medals, very often with the Lamb as part of the design.

While the gold reliquary is very grand (such items are not particularly common), the most significant item is probably the silver-gilt cover with an 'A' mounted inside the handle. This is not, as was thought, the cover of an inkwell, but the lid of an altar-cruet, the 'A' standing for '*Aqua*' (water). Oddly enough similar items are relatively common from Spanish wrecks. From the wrecked treasure galleon of 1641, *Nuestra Senora de la Pura y Limpia Concepcion*, comes a similar lid bearing an 'A', except that in this case the letter is horizontal rather than vertical. The altar-cruet for water implies the existence of another with a 'V' for '*Vinum*' (wine) and the *Nuestra Senora de Atocha*, wrecked in a storm with the loss of 260 lives on a Florida reef in 1622, produced two cruets marked with 'V's. Also from the *Nuestra Senora de Atocha* came what is very likely to have been a paten, in richly engraved gold. The presence on board of either of the altar-cruets does imply that there should have been a complete set of altar-plate, at least a chalice and paten. It is likely that among the retinue of Don Alonso de Leiva there could have been one of the 180 or so clerics who sailed with the Armada. It is, of course, possible that the cruet could also have belonged to the Bishop of Killaloe, in the time before a considerable amount of Irish altar-plate of pre-Reformation date was either melted down or taken for refuge to the Continent – where it was completely lost to posterity.

Sources used for Chapter 12

Fallon, N., *The Armada in Ireland*, London, 1978
Flanagan, L., Martin, C. and Stenuit, R., *Tresors de l'Armada*, Brussels, 1985
Hackenbrock, Y., *Smalti e Gioielli*, Florence, 1986
Martin, C., *Full Fathom Five*, London, 1975
Mathewson, R.D., *Treasure of the Atocha*, London, 1986
Maxwell, C., *Irish History from Contemporary Sources, 1509–1610*, London, 1923
Muller, P., *Jewels in Spain 1500–1800*, New York, 1972
Oman, C., *The Golden Age of Hispanic Silver*, London, 1968
Peterson, M., *Treasure of the Concepcion*, Chicago, 1980
Stenuit, R., *Treasures of the Armada*, London, 1972

Religion

12.1 CRUCIFIX, Silver
68mm h; 10.90g
A badly eroded silver Crucifix; only the decapitated Body and the right Arm survive, with the right arm of the Cross
Girona

12.2 CRUCIFIX, Bronze
81mm h
Simple bronze Cross, the arms and
the foot end in points; there is a
suspension loop at the top. The
figure of Christ is missing. The
letters *INRI* are inscribed on a
horizontal band near the top; at the
foot is a skull in relief
Girona

12.3 FIGURE FROM A CRUCIFIX, Gilt Bronze
26mm l
Badly abraded figure of Christ; the
two arms are missing and the gilding
survives only on the chest and the
sides of the legs
Girona

12.4 RING, Gold
27mm d; 6.93g
Heavy gold ring with a circular bezel
on which are the letters *IHS* (the
Sacred Monogram), surmounted by
a cross. Beneath the monogram is a
single nail of the Cross. Since the
monogram was adopted by the
Society of Jesus, it is possible that
this ring belonged to a Jesuit on
board
Girona

12.5 *AGNUS DEI* RELIQUARY, Gold
39mm h; 51.21g
Gold box in the form of a book; the
hinged lid is decorated in relief, with
a central area framed by pillars and
topped with a pediment containing a
representation of St John the

Baptist. The interior is divided into five circular compartments, with a central raised portion corresponding to a receptacle accessed from the back, presumably originally containing a relic over which a cover, held in place by the same sort of architectural frame as appears on the front, fitted. When found the receptacle contained little wax tablets, identified as *Agnus Dei*, made from the wax of Paschal candles, blessed by the Pope, believed to be endowed with protective properties (see colour plate)
Girona

12.6 RELIGIOUS MEDAL, Copper
31mm l
Small oval medal with a suspension loop at the top and three little lugs. On one face is the Madonna and Child, on the other the Head of Christ and the inscription *SALVAM TE* (That I may save thee)
La Trinidad Valencera

12.7 RELIGIOUS MEDAL, Pewter
32mm l
Small oval religious medal with a suspension loop at the top; on one face is the Madonna and Child, on the other the Head of Christ and an indecipherable inscription
La Trinidad Valencera

12.8 RELIGIOUS MEDAL, Pewter
38mm l
Small oval medal with on one face the Crucifixion and on the other the Madonna and Child
Girona

12.9 RELIGIOUS MEDAL, Pewter
40mm l
As above but with the Head of
Christ on one side and the Virgin's
head on the other
Girona

12.10 RELIGIOUS MEDAL, Pewter
42 mm l
As above
Girona

12.11 RELIGIOUS MEDAL, Pewter
37mm l
As above
Girona

12.12 RELIGIOUS MEDAL, Pewter
37mm l
As 12.8 above
Girona

12.13 RELIGIOUS MEDAL, Copper
25mm l
The Madonna and Child and (?) St
Anne on one face, the Crucifixion on
the other
Girona

12.14 LID OF AN ALTAR CRUET, Silver gilt
40mm d; 53.29g
A flat circular lid, decorated on top
with concentric circles. On the top is
an 'A' in a circle; the A is for *Aqua*
(Water) and the lid that of an Altar
Cruet or Ewer, implying the
existence of a corresponding vessel
with a V for *Vinum* (Wine), but also
of at least a Chalice and Paten
Girona

CHAPTER 13
Jewellery

Among the finds from the *Girona* was an unparalleled collection of Renaissance jewellery. This may seem surprising until it is recalled that the Armada was an invasion force and the Spanish officers and nobility on board had every intention of looking their very best when strutting, victorious, through the streets of London.

The jewellery falls into two classes: that with a specifically honorific element – the badges of Orders of Chivalry; and that with a totally decorative function, or worn as an expression of conspicuous consumption. Both are well represented.

In sixteenth-century Spain there were three major native Orders of Chivalry: Compostela, Calatrava and Alcantara, all originally founded as religious military orders, whose main purpose was to fight the Moors in Spain. Of these the badges of two are represented among the *Girona* collection. By far the most important is the badge of a Knight of the Order of Santiago de Compostela, for it belonged to Don Alonso de Leiva, one of the most respected commanders in the Armada and selected by Phillip II as Commander-designate in the event of the death of Medina Sidonia. This Order was traditionally founded in the tenth century to commemorate a victory over the Moors and was confirmed in 1175 by Pope Alexander III. The wars against the Moors enhanced both the reputation and the wealth of the Order and its Grand-Mastership was vested permanently in the Spanish Crown by Pope Adrian VI in 1522.

Santiago de Compostela was, in the Middle Ages, one of the most famous shrines in Europe, for there was entombed the body of St James the Great (Santiago = St James). Among those who made the pilgrimage were many Irish people; for example, in 1445, 'Many of the Irish of Ireland went towards the City of St James the Apostle to Spain in that summer' and 'returned safe and sound to their own houses in Ireland after receiving the Indulgences of St James.' The Badge of the Order of Santiago de Compostela is the red lily-hilted sword of St James. The gold Cross recovered from the *Girona* site is precisely this design, with traces of the red enamel preserved, framed in a gold oval with a loop and ring for suspension from a chain or ribbon (Cat 13.4).

Don Alonso de Leiva, to whom this Cross belonged, was a former Captain-General of the Galleys of Naples and Captain-General of the Milanese Light Infantry; a man of considerable military and naval experience. He had been critical of the pace with which the Marquis of Santa Cruz had conducted the preparations for the Armada and was equally critical of the Duke of Medina Sidonia during the fighting in the Channel, when he himself was in command of *La Rata Sancta Maria Encoronada*. He is recorded as exclaiming, 'His Majesty has given a man to command us at sea who looks as if he wouldn't know how to walk on dry land.' For all his natural ability and experience as a commander, de Leiva's own ship was the first to be wrecked on the Irish coast, at Blacksod Bay, Co. Mayo. He systematically stripped the grounded vessel of everything that could be salvaged and then set fire to the hull, fortifying his position at nearby Fahy Castle until he learned of another Spanish ship nearby, the *Duquesa Santa Ana*, under the command of Don Pedro Mores. De Leiva and his men embarked on the *Duquesa Santa Ana*, only to be wrecked a second time at Loughros More, Co. Donegal. Here once more he showed his determination to make the best of his situation; he removed as much as possible from the stricken ship and, although injured by a capstan in the process, again created a fortified camp for himself and his surviving men. This time it lay on an island in Kiltoorish Lake, where some 380 years later Robert Stenuit discovered an iron falcon from the ship used as part of the defences of the camp. It was here that he heard that the galleass *Girona* was in harbour at Killybegs, some twenty miles away overland. Because of his injury de Leiva himself had to be carried on a litter. Arriving at Killybegs, he carried out the repairs necessary to the *Girona* – her rudder had been damaged – possibly cannibalising two other small ships also at Killybegs. Then he set off again, sailing first north and then east to try to reach Scotland and thence the Continent. Unfortunately the cruel talon of rock that is Lacada Point, Co. Antrim, lay in his way and here he was wrecked for the third and final time; his Cross of a Knight of Santiago was to be found nearly four hundred years later to prove the truth of the document that claimed he had perished here.

This document is the letter written in Antwerp in 1589 by Captain Francisco de Cuellar, survivor of a Streedagh wreck, who, after many adventures crossing Ireland, 'reached the place where Don Alonso de Leiva, the Conde de Paredes and Don Tomas de Granvela had perished'. He also mentions that he was shown many jewels and valuables that had belonged to those who died on the *Girona*, which suggests that those recovered by twentieth-century diving may be only a small fraction of those originally on board. A portrait by El Greco, now in Montreal, described as either 'a member of the de Leiva family' or 'a Knight of the Order of Santiago' was thought at one time to be a portrait of this Don Alonso de Leiva. However, the subject of the portrait is dark-haired and of a rather sallow complexion, while the Commander-designate of the Armada is described by his contemporaries as 'flaxen-haired and fair-complexioned'. It seems unlikely, therefore, that he is in fact the subject, an unfortunate conclusion, since good, contemporary portraits of the Spanish commanders are few in number.

The other Spanish Order of Chivalry represented among the material recovered from the *Girona* is a Cross of a Knight of Alcantara (Cat 13.3). This Order was established about 1156 and, because there was a hermitage nearby, surrounded by wild pear trees and dedicated to Saint Julian, its members were known at first as Knights of St Julian of the Pear-tree. When the defence of Alcantara, recently recovered from the Moors, was entrusted to them, they took the name of the Order from that city. Like the Order of Santiago they prospered and, in due course, saw their Grand-Mastership taken over by the King. Again that arrangement was made permanent by Pope Adrian VI in 1523.

The Cross of Alcantara is in the form of a small receptacle. One side, forming the lid, carries a fine engraving of a long-haired, bearded saint, behind whom is a stylised tree. The saint is manifestly St Julian, the tree equally a pear-tree. Also in the picture is a waterfall, which commemorates one of the most famous miracles performed by St Julian, who lived in the fourth century. The other side, of which none of the coloured enamel has survived, forms the body of an openwork cross, each terminal ending in a fleur-de-lys – the Cross fleury that is appropriate to the Order. Unfortunately the identity of the owner of this fine Cross has obstinately remained a mystery.

In addition to the Crosses of these Spanish Orders, the wreck-site of the *Girona* yielded another Knight's Cross: that from the Order of the Hospital of St John of Jerusalem (Cat 13.2). This Order was founded in the eleventh century as a medical order, to care for pilgrims making their way to the Holy Land. The original hospice, purchased by some merchants from Amalfi, was served by Benedictines and was later dedicated to St John the Baptist. When, in 1087, the Crusaders surrounded Jerusalem, the then head of the hospital, a man known only as Gerard, was of great assistance to them. According to one legend he had joined the Saracen defenders of the City on the walls, but, instead of throwing stones, he threw loaves of bread at the Christian Crusaders, who were short of food. When he was accused of assisting the attackers, the loaves which he had thrown and which were produced as evidence had miraculously been turned into stones. Whatever the aid given, the gratitude of the Christians afterwards was almost unbounded; donations and privileges were showered upon the hospital by kings, nobles and prelates in France, Spain, Portugal, England and Italy. In 1113, Pope Paschal II took the Order and its possessions under his immediate protection.

The Knights Hospitaller devoted themselves primarily to the medical care of the sick, and the building of hospitals around Jerusalem and along the main pilgrimage routes. However, the constant need to protect the pilgrims forced them to adopt a military role as well and they became increasingly involved in military activities. Eventually, in 1291, the Christians and the Knights were virtually forced to retire from the Holy Land, first to Cyprus and then to Rhodes. Here they settled, well-established by 1310, and the buildings of their hospital and fortress are still to be seen. It was a commanding position, dominating the seaways from east to west, and their preoccupations became somewhat more commerical and less religious, though they did still maintain their network of hospitals. They also delayed for some two centuries the appearance of the Ottomans as a formidable naval power, until, in 1522, the Knights were expelled from Rhodes by Suleiman the Magnificent. During their period on Rhodes, the Order had been wholly international and was organised into *langues*, or tongues – of Auvergne, Provence, France, Aragon, Castile, Portugal, England, Germany and Italy. It was a united front line in the defence of Europe.

When the Knights were expelled from Rhodes, Charles V of Spain granted them the island of Malta in 1530 and from then on they became known less formally as Knights of Malta, and their badge, therefore, a 'Maltese Cross'. They now owed their territory to Spain, although, when Malta was under siege by Suleiman and his forces, Spain was remarkably dilatory in sending assistance. Notwithstanding, at the great naval battle of Lepanto in 1571, when the Spanish and Venetians inflicted a resounding defeat on the Turks, the Knights were deeply involved, throwing in their considerable strength on the side of Christendom.

The Armada, however, posed rather a problem for members of the Order. Henry VIII had confiscated their English possessions, their English *langue* no longer existed, Elizabeth had been excommunicated and the English were heretics; but despite all this, the Knights were forbidden to bear arms against a Christian prince. On the other hand, after their equivalent of 'military service' to the Order, members went 'on the Reserve' and could not, as individuals, refuse to accept their sovereign's command to fight against his focs. The owner of the Cross of a Knight of St John found on the *Girona* site must, therefore, have been in something of a quandary, but he obviously had accepted Philip II's summons and had taken his prestigious Cross with him, to his death at Lacada Point. Here Robert Stenuit found it, nearly 400 years later: a gold Maltese Cross, some 60mm high, the surface keyed for white enamel, some small traces of which survive. Between the arms of the Cross are motifs similar to small fleur-de-lys. Stenuit has suggested that these are little spines and has taken them as a heraldic proof of the fact that the Cross originally belonged to Fabricio Spinola of Genoa, the captain of the *Girona*. We know he was the captain because, against the entry for the *Girona* in a copy of the Armada Inventory that belonged to Lord Burghley, Elizabeth's Secretary of State, are written the words 'perished on the coast of Ireland', as well as 'Fabricio Spinola Captn'. One possible objection is that many Crosses of the Order, whose owners had no conceivable connection with the Spinola family, have similar motifs between the arms of the Cross; however, this does not necessarily invalidate the supposition that this Cross did, in fact, belong to Fabricio Spinola.

Such badges of Orders of Chivalry could be worn round the neck suspended either from a ribbon of the appropriate colour or from a chain of gold. The chain could either be a simple link-chain, such as is often seen round the necks of gentlemen in Renaissance portraits, or a composite chain, con-structed of elaborately wrought and jewelled elements, all linked together. Both types were found on the wreck-site of the *Girona*. Two simple chains of quite massive proportions and, consequently, value were recovered: one of over a metre long and weighing 393g, the other over two metres long and weighing a mighty 818g (Cat 13.5–13.6). Such chains as these, even in the sixteenth century, were not merely conspicuous, but spectacular displays of wealth. They had the advantage that, in times of need, a link or two could be detached to pay for goods or services. Perhaps it was for this reason that these large plain chains were made of simple butt-jointed, oval links which would make the detachment of one or two relatively simple. However, many of the owners of these from the Armada who did not drown, as presumably those of the two *Girona* chains did, fell victim to a crowd either of impoverished Irish or of English anxious for their position if the Spanish should land in force on a scantily defended Ireland. Either way, reaching the shore did not profit the Spanish greatly; in addition to reports of the butchery of Spanish survivors and the subsequent pillaging of valuables from their bodies, there are reports of the circulation in the north of Ireland, in the years immediately subsequent to the Armada, of gold chains almost certainly obtained in this fashion.

In addition to the large and heavy chains from the *Girona*, there is a group of four finer and lighter chains. Three of these are made in a similar fashion, composed of simple oval links, but with each link passing through four others, giving a continuous flowing effect. One of them has two knots, presumably to shorten it. The fourth light chain is composed of small, flat figures of eight, each twisted at the middle (Cat 13.8). These fine chains, now ranging from a mere 25cm to nearly 75cm, could also have been used to hang badges of chivalry; they do not however possess either the advantages or disadvantages of the larger heavier chains.

Sometimes, of course, more elaborate composite chains were used to suspend badges of Orders of Chivalry; one from the *Girona* is composed of three different sorts of element, all of gold. One of the larger elements is more or less rectangular, about 21mm long, with a circular hole in the centre. This would have contained a stone or more probably a pearl, for the fine gold wire to hold it in position is still extant. At each end is a small hole, through which a bent figure-of-eight link passed to connect this to the next element. That would have been a simple connecting-piece, almost hour-glass shape, with fine pellet-decoration around the edges and a B-shaped link on the back. The third kind of element is more elaborate: instead of a simple central hole, a hollow gold truncated conical mount arises, with a setting for a gem that has not survived. This mount is held in place by a small gold strap with a gold rivet and collar; on the strap is inscribed 'XII', but the meaning of the inscription is not at the moment clear. The whole assemblage would have made a very pleasing composite chain of which nine elements survive; the nature of the links was designed to let the chain lie flat (Cat 13.18). Queen Elizabeth of England had a similar chain, similarly with three different kinds of element among its twenty-three pieces: ten with two pearls apiece, two with one pearl a piece and eleven with representations of men and animals. Interestingly enough, in England it was not customary for any except royalty to wear the 'George' of the Order of the Garter on a chain or collar embellished with precious stones.

Another kind of necklace is a collection of lapis lazuli portrait-cameos, in gold frames with pearls (Cat 13.25). From the twelve thought to originally exist, the remains of eleven survive in varying degrees of completeness. The most complete, in almost its original condition, retains not only its lapis lazuli portrait, in a very fresh blue, but also on either side the frame still has the four matched pearls, strung on a fine gold wire, presumed to be its original complement. On each shoulder of the frame is a small setting filled with green enamel. The top of the frame consists of a grotesque mask, supported on scrolls. The cameo itself is backed by an oval plate of gold, held in place by tiny triangular gold teeth, bent alternately. The rings for the connecting-links on the back show clearly that the cameos were intended to be worn one above the other rather than side-by-side: the upper ring runs along the long axis, while the lower ring is set at right-angles to it. Presumably six were worn on each side. Six of the actual cameos survive, a further four frames contain only the back-plate and the eleventh consists only of the frame. Controversy surrounds the identification of the emperors depicted. Robert Stenuit, after exhaustive searches among representations of Roman emperors became convinced that these were of the Byzantine period and included Stauratius, Michael I Rhangabe and Constantine II, though this has been disputed. Such confusion about the identities of Romans in Renaissance jewellery is not unusual. A set of twelve cameos in Vienna depicts Roman emperors, with the name of the emperor inscribed in black enamel on the frame, but the portraits are not correctly matched with the names.

A selection of other gold frames, which may originally have contained cameos, was also found on the *Girona*. Several different styles are present (Cat 13.20–13.23) The most splendid is a single find, consisting of a heavy oval frame of gold, with relief ornament all round and pellet-decoration round the opening. A set of six lozenge-shaped mounts, with oval openings, retaining the tooth-shaped clips to hold the missing cameos or intaglios, and another trio of gold mounts, oval in outline and again with only the clips surviving, may represent composite chains, hat-bands or bracelets. Another composite chain connected by gold links may also be shown by a pair of gold ornaments with perforations at both ends; each ornament is set with two pearls on either side of a central raised square mount, which in one example retains a table-cut ruby. A final frame among the jewellery recovered from the *Girona* is quite different. Unfortunately it is sadly deformed from its original oval shape, but two decorative features survive. One of these is a shouldered mount of gold still retaining a small ruby; a single triangular tooth also survives from the series that would have held in place the framed feature (Cat 13.24).

Perhaps, at first sight even more surprising than this jewellery, is the selection of rings recovered. One is particularly interesting, for it constituted the first conclusive evidence that the site at Lacada Point was veritably that of the *Girona* and not any other unrecorded Armada wreck.

This is a rather large and simple gold ring, obviously intended to be worn by a man. It has a crushed rectangular bezel, now lacking its stone, and the ring is inscribed *Madame de Champagney MDXXIIII* (Cat 13.13). When Stenuit discovered this ring his first reaction was, quite naturally, one of puzzlement: what on earth was a ring with an inscription referring to a woman and bearing the date 1524 doing on an Armada wreck? Patient detective work on his part eventually unravelled the mystery. The name 'Champagney' was the first clue: this led to the fact that in 1588 the manor of Champagney, near Besançon, was in the possession of Frederick Perrenot. He was not involved in the Armada, nor could the inscription on the ring refer to his wife Constance, for she was not even born in 1524; the ring, therefore, must have been an heirloom. It transpired that Frederick had inherited the lands of Champagney from his brother Jerome, who, in his turn, had inherited them from his father, Nicolas. By Nicolas they had been received as a dowry on his marriage to Nicole Bonvalot of Besançon. Among the eleven children of Nicolas and Nicole was Jerome, who, as luck would have it, was actually born in 1524. It looks, therefore, as if the ring was originally worn by Nicolas Perrenot (and also de Granvelle) in honour of his wife on the occasion of the birth of their second son. Thus it seems it was Jean-Thomas, the son of Jerome and the grandson of the 'Madame de Champagney' referred to on the ring, who was wearing it when the *Girona* sank at Lacada Point in 1588. His Armada career is fairly well documented: he is listed as one of those who embarked on *La Rata Sancta Maria Encoronada*, along with Don Alonso de

Leiva; with de Leiva he transferred to the *Duquesa Santa Ana* after the first wreck in Blacksod Bay, and again with him to the *Girona* after the wreck at Loughros More, Co. Donegal. Finally, they perished together at Lacada Point, as was testified by Francisco de Cuellar.

While the secure knowledge that the 22-year-old Don Tomas Perrenoto was one of those to meet his death at Lacada Point is poignant, another ring recovered has a similar effect. It is a small gold ring, now open between the terminals, one of which consists of a hand clasping a heart, the other a buckle. It bears the inscription '*No tengo mas que dar te*' ('I have nothing more to give thee') and was quite patently a parting present to one of those on board from his true love (Cat 13.11). We shall never know for certain who this hapless soul was, nor the identity of his love, but this little gift illumines, as perhaps nothing else can, the thousands of personal and family tragedies that the Armada story contains.

Not all the rings recovered were the adits to such mines of historical information or such emotional indicators. Some were, quite simply, handsome pieces of jewellery. One of the better preserved is a large gold ring, whose bezel is badly crushed but retains one of its complement of diamonds; both shoulders have settings for diamonds and again one survives. Of three badly crushed rings, two have bezels which originally were set with a large central gem and four small ones, none of which have survived. The other had a single stone, no longer present, with the bezel decorated with pellets. Another ring, among the best preserved, has a finely modelled figure of a salamander in full relief as its bezel; each shoulder is decorated with a small human face (Cat 13.12).

Representations of fabulous creatures, whether entirely mythological, like the fire-resistant salamander, or the exotic perceived in the farthermost regions of the Spanish World, were quite common elements in Spanish jewellery. The New World of the Americas had revealed not only the exquisite craftsmanship in precious metals of the Indians, but also a menagerie of exotic animals to be added to those observed in the Pacific. There is, therefore, sometimes a little doubt whether a creature on a jewel is 'real' or 'imaginary'. This dilemma is best seen in what is probably the most magnificent piece of jewellery from the *Girona* – an exquisitely modelled gold salamander-pendant set with rubies (Cat 13.1). Originally there were nine of these table-cut stones; sadly only three survive. The creature is a mere 42mm long, but every scale, on its back, stomach, four legs and even on its curved tail, is carefully delineated. Its eyes, with eyebrows, its nose, mouth with little teeth and even tongue are all shown, as are its webbed feet. From its two sides sprout a pair of wings and round the neck there appears to be a small collar. Is this the mythical salamander, referred to in the first century by Pliny, which not only could survive the fire, but extinguish it? Or is it on the other hand, as some would suggest, a representation of the flying lizard, *Draco volans*, known from the East Indies and Philippines, where a Spanish colony had been established in 1565. Either interpretation is valid; Francis I had adopted the salamander as his badge, and the accompanying motto '*Nutrisco et extinguo*' ('I nourish and extinguish') makes it quite clear that this was no mere lizard. Other ambiguous creatures include the pelican, which could be regarded as either simply a bird or as a symbol of Christ, for the pelican biting her breast to feed her young was commonly so used in the Middle Ages. Similarly a frog-pendant could be seen either as depicting a frog or as carrying the symbolism with which the animal was endowed by the natives of America; to the Aztecs it represented the rain god, while to some South American Indian tribes it represented poison. On the other hand, among the jewelled pendants of sixteenth-century Spain are numerous representations of exotic creatures: turtles, parrots, crayfish – all basically naturalistic, albeit bearing jewels.

The salamander-pendant from the *Girona* interestingly bears its nine rubies in the form of a cross, the top being on the reptile's head, the base just above its tail and the arms just on its shoulders. On the underside of each wing is a small ring for attaching a suspension chain; in one a single circular link survives in place. Now separated from the pendant is the little fitting from which it hung: a small more or less triangular body, carrying a single ruby, it has the major suspension loop at its apex, by which the whole pendant would hang from its chain. From each side of the base of the triangle comes a little chain consisting of alternate circular links of fine gold wire and fine little bars with circular terminals engaging in the links.

One rather interesting item in the *Girona* collection is a gold combined ear- and tooth-pick in the form of a dolphin (Cat 13.26).However, it is perhaps difficult for a modern mind to accept the very concept of such a device, and probably even more difficult to contemplate actually using it.

Among the miscellaneous items from the range of jewellery found on the *Girona* site is one particularly attractive piece: a rosette of fine gold filigree. Badly crushed when it was found, it was, after careful straightening by a goldsmith, revealed as an almost perfect twelve-rayed rosette, each ray or segment elaborately worked in fine gold wire, with a circular centre-piece (Cat 13.27). Several other fragments of equally fine filigree work were also recovered, as were additional pieces of fine gold chains; indeed several tiny individual links of fine gold chain were found, which, considering the conditions under which work was carried out at Lacada Point, is a testimony to the skill and observation of the divers.

One of the important features of the jewellery from the *Girona* is that it constitutes a large, closely dated find of Renaissance jewellery; so closely dated is it, that the presence of heirlooms, like the 'Madame de Champagney' ring, is immediately detectable. From a hoard of this size and magnificence a great deal can be learned of the sixteenth-century jeweller's art and craft and, more generally, of trade and commerce of the period.

The first question to ask is where did all the gold come from? While the 'Madame de Champagney' ring, for example, weighs a mere 6.24g, and even the Cross of a Knight of Malta only 37g, the two heavier gold chains together weigh almost 1.25kg, which, by any consideration, is a large amount of gold. Their value, simply as bullion, would in the present day market be in the region of £20,000.

There are many places in Europe and the Near and Middle East where gold occurs and was exploited in prehistoric and Roman times; deposits in Anatolia, Egypt, Greece, Yugoslavia, Iberia and the British Isles were exploited throughout the Bronze and Iron Ages, and some of these sources continued to be worked through the Roman period and even into the Middle Ages. By the sixteenth century, however, many of these sources had been either totally worked out or what gold remained was too difficult to extract with the technologies then available.

By this period Europe was increasingly dependent for gold supplies on the mines of Africa: sources such as Sofala, inland of Mombasa on the East African coast; Taqcrour in the western Sudan, which is recorded as providing two caravans a year; Guinea in West Africa (hence the name 'Gold Coast' for this area), which was producing about 700kg a year in the early part of the sixteenth century. However, by the end of the century, access to East Africa was becoming more hazardous for the Portuguese, who were its main exploiters. At first this was the result of interference with the trade-route to Persia and India by the Turks; then, in 1589, disruption was caused by a fierce rebellion by the black inhabitants of the entire coast. It was, therefore, fortunate for the jewellers of Spain and the rest of Europe that other supplies were available from the transatlantic New World. By the mid-sixteenth century more than four tons of gold a year was coming across the Atlantic, nearly six times the output of the Gold Coast. The regulations applied by the *Casa de Contratacion* to the silver trade applied equally to the trade in gold; all the legally traded gold was stamped to indicate its weight and its purity. From the meticulous records maintained by the *Casa*, and from those that survive in the *Archivo General de Indias*, we know that *La Santa Maria de Yciar* one of the wrecks off Padre Island excavated by the Texas Antiquities Committee, was 'officially' carrying 1,148 pesos of 18 carat gold. The excavations on the site, however, recovered two bars of gold, each duly stamped, one stamp indicating fineness (15.5 and 15.75 carats respectively), and one to confirm that they are of gold. The discrepancy between the gold in the manifest and that found on the wreck-site may be evidence of smuggling, despite the penalties; it may, on the other hand, indicate that the wreck was not that of *La Santa Maria de Yciar*.

We know, therefore, that much of the gold used in the *Girona* jewellery is likely to have come from the New World. Unfortunately not enough work investigating the possibility of source identification of such gold by means of trace elements has yet been carried out to confirm this; however, the assumption of its provenance remains.

The next problem to be discussed is the source of the precious and semi-precious stones used in the *Girona* jewellery. Both rubies and diamonds are present. The source of the diamonds is relatively simple, because, until the discovery of diamonds in Brazil in 1725 and in South Africa in 1867, the only major source of diamonds was in five areas in India, which had certainly been worked in the Middle Ages. Until Vasco de Gama first sailed the sea passage to India in 1498, these Indian diamonds reached Europe by two overland routes: a northern one, passing through Constantinople; and a southern one through Cairo. From these two places they were transported to Venice, the principal centre for the luxury trade with the East. They were then traded mainly to Antwerp, in the form of rough stones, for finishing, and to Lisbon and Paris. It was in the sixteenth century that Antwerp expanded as a finishing centre, later, but gradually, to be replaced by Amsterdam.

The rubies present are likely to have come from a limited number of sources, in Burma, Thailand, Cambodia, Ceylon and Afghanistan. On mineralogical grounds, those used in the *Girona* salamander-pendant are probably of Burmese origin, but any of the sources listed was possible commercially. The lapis lazuli in the portrait-cameos is most likely to have come from Afghanistan, where the deposits on the Kokcha River have been worked since prehistoric times.

The pearls could have come from several systematic pearl-fisheries in the Old World. Pearling was carried out in the Red Sea and Persian Gulf, controlled by the Arabs, and off the north-east of Ceylon, and the yield exported to Europe along routes common to other luxuries from the East. As with gold, however, Spain was to obtain a new source in the Americas, where pearls had been fished near Trinidad and exported to that country even before the Spanish Conquest.

That jewellery-making was taken very seriously in the sixteenth century is shown by the number of books of jewellers' designs that survive, notably in the *Libres de Passanties* preserved in Barcelona, although similar books are preserved elsewhere. All goldsmiths' guilds required that an apprentice pass various tests, both theoretical and practical, before qualifying as a master. These volumes contain designs submitted for such tests, but other designs survive, including some by Holbein.

The techniques used by Renaissance jewellers include casting, the drawing of fine wires, engraving, enamelling and many other modes of fabrication as well as the setting of gems and semi-precious stones. Pearls, being easy to drill, were usually strung on fine gold wires. The harder gem-stones, many of them with the minimum amount of finishing and virtually in their natural state, albeit polished, were usually mounted in fairly simple settings, notably the so-called 'bowl-setting'. In this a small golden bowl was fashioned to receive the gem, usually of rectangular cut; then the rim of the bowl was pressed laterally to help hold the stone in place. All these techniques are to be seen among the jewels from the *Girona*, as part of a fair representation of sixteenth-century taste in jewellery.

It must be remembered that as far as jewellery was concerned Renaissance Man's choice was intended to indicate the wearer's status as well as his taste; this is revealed in a recorded observation that, when Lucrezia Borgia went to Ferrara, seventy-five of the Duke of Ferrara's gentlemen wore chains 'none of which cost less than 500 ducats'. Men, as well as women, wore rings, bracelets, hat-jewels – even jewelled armour. The *Girona* collection gives us an additional insight into this jewel-conscious society.

Sources used for Chapter 13

Calendar of State Papers (Ireland), 1588–1605

Flanagan, L., Martin, C. and Stenuit, R., *Tresors de l'Armada*, Brussels, 1985

Hackenbrock, Y., *Smalti e Gioielli*, Florence, 1986

Muller, P., *Jewels in Spain 1500–1800*, New York, 1972

O'Donovan, J., 'The Annals of Ireland from the Year 1443 to 1468', *Miscellany of the Irish Archaeol. Soc.*, (1) 1846

O'Reilly, J.P., 'Captain Cuellar's Narrative', *Proc. Roy. Irish Acad.*, 1893

Palache, C., Berman, H. and Frondel, C., *Dana's System of Mineralogy*, New York, 1966

Stenuit, R., *Treasures of the Armada*, London, 1972

Tait, H., *Jewellery through 7,000 Years*, London, 1976

Jewellery

13.1 SALAMANDER PENDANT,
Gold and Rubies
42mm l; 19.55g
Gold pendant in the form of a salamander, with four legs and two wings; the scales, mouth, teeth, eyes and nose are clearly modelled. Of the nine table-cut and bowl-set

rubies only three survive. A little
suspension-fitting of gold chain with
a ruby-set mount was originally
attached to two loops on the
underside of the wings (see colour
plate)
Girona

13.2 CROSS OF THE ORDER OF ST JOHN, Gold and white enamel
60mm h; 36.90g
Gold 'Maltese' Cross, each arm
divided into two points; at the top is
a suspension loop carrying a spiral of
gold wire. Between each arm of the
Cross is a small fleur-de-lys-like
motif. The surface is keyed for
white enamel, a small amount of
which is extant. Belonged to
Fabricio Spinola, Captain of the
Girona
Girona

13.3 CROSS OF THE ORDER OF ALCANTARA, Gold
28mm h; 10.81g
Knight's Cross in the form of a
receptacle; the body consists of an
oval containing a fretted Cross, each
arm terminating in a fleur-de-lys;
there is a small suspension-loop at
the top. The lid, which fits tightly,
bears a representation of a long-
haired, bearded Saint, with a tree in
the background; the Saint is St
Julien, the tree a pear-tree. The
owner has not been identified
Girona

**13.4 CROSS OF THE ORDER OF
SANTIAGO, Gold and red enamel**
44mm l; 11.92g
Oval frame containing a fretted
Cross in the form of a sword with
the hilt in the form of an inverted
heart, the arms terminating in fleurs-
de-lys. The surface of the Cross is
keyed for red enamel, a portion of
which survives. There is a
suspension-loop at the top. This
Cross belonged to Don Alonso de
Leiva, Commander-Designate of the
Armada (see colour plate)
Girona

13.5 CHAIN, Gold
1220mm l; 392.66g
Heavy gold chain consisting of 136
links, 13mm long, of 2mm thick
gold wire, butt-jointed; some of the
joints are slightly open (inside chain
in picture)
Girona

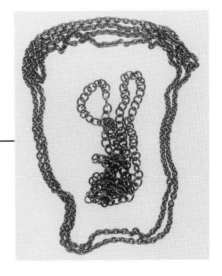

13.6 CHAIN, Gold
2300mm l; 817.58g
Simple gold chain of 407 links,
10mm long, of 25mm thick gold
wire, butt-jointed (outside chain in
picture)
Girona

13.7 CHAIN, Gold
495mm l; 19.55g
Length of fine gold chain composed
of links 4mm long; each link passes
through 4 others
Girona

13.8 CHAIN, Gold
228mm l; 4.68g
Length of fine gold chain consisting
of flat gold links of figure-of-eight
shape, 6mm l, twisted at the
crossing
Girona

13.9 CHAIN, Gold
808mm l; 14.16g
Length of fine gold chain consisting
of links 4mm long; each link passes
through 4 others
Girona

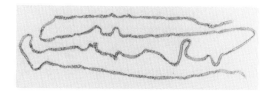

13.10 CHAIN, Gold
215mm+ l; 11.04g
Length of fine gold chain consisting
of oval links 5mm long, each passing
through 4 others; there are two
knots in the chain, presumably to
shorten it
Girona

13.11 RING, Gold
21mm d; 2.59g
Small gold ring with one terminal in
the form of a hand holding a heart,
the other a buckle; it is inscribed *No
tengo mas que dar te* (I have nothing
more to give thee)
Girona

13.12 RING, Gold
24mm d; 3.25g
Gold ring with rectangular bezel on
which is mounted a relief figure of a
Salamander; each shoulder of the
bezel has a small human head
Girona

13.13 RING, Gold
27mm d; 6.24g
Large gold ring with a rectangular
bezel and setting for a gem-stone no
longer present. It is inscribed
Madame de Champagney MDXXIIII
(1524). It was worn by Madame's
grandson, Don Tomas Perrenoto,
when he perished at Lacada Point
Girona

13.14 RING, Gold with Diamonds
25mm d; 6.14g
Gold ring with crushed bezel divided
into four settings, in one of which a
diamond survives; each shoulder has
three small settings in one of which
a diamond survives
Girona

13.15 RING, Gold
25mm d; 3.95g
Badly crushed gold ring; the crushed
bezel had a setting for one large
central stone and four smaller; each
shoulder also has a setting; none of
the stones now survives. The hoop is
decorated with lozenges in low relief
Girona

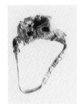

13.16 RING, Gold
25mm d; 5.47g
Gold ring with badly crushed bezel
which had a setting for one central
stone and four others, none of which
has survived. The hoop is decorated
with alternating ovals and lozenges
in low relief
Girona

13.17 RING, Gold

30mm d; 4.95g

Badly crushed gold ring; the bezel,
now empty, had a setting for a
single stone, the edges with pellet-
decoration
Girona

13.18 COMPOSITE CHAIN, Gold

85mm+ l; 14.37g

A composite chain consisting of
three different types of element: one
is more or less rectangular, 21mm l,
with a circular opening in the
centre, over which passes a fine gold
wire suggesting that it contained a
pearl; at each end is a hole to take a
gold link to connect to the next
element. The next type is a variant
of the first: instead of a simple hole,
the centre bears a little mount in the
form of a truncated pyramid, the
bowl setting for a gem. The third
type of element is a simple narrow
bar, 6mm wide; on the back is a
connector in the form of the letter
'B' to which the links from the other
elements would attach
Girona

13.19 COMPOSITE CHAIN, Gold
with Pearls and Rubies

28mm l; 5.58g (each)

Two elements of a composite chain,
each more or less oval in outline,
with a central raised square setting,
in one of which a ruby survives; on
each side is a pearl held in place by
a fine gold wire. At each end is a
hole to receive a connecting link
Girona

13.20 MOUNT, Gold
29mm h; 11.99g
Composite oval mount, consisting of
a heavy gold frame, with relief-
decoration at the top, bottom and
sides, inside which has been
soldered a raised collar, decorated
with pellets, which probably
contained a cameo or intaglio
Girona

13.21 MOUNTS, Gold
24mm h; 2.14g (each)
Six little oval mounts with oval
openings in the centre, with a slight
raised collar, in which was probably
mounted a cameo or intaglio, held in
place by the little triangular gold
teeth which survive – in different
numbers – round the edges of the
openings
Girona

13.22 MOUNTS, Gold
30mm h; 2.54g (each)
Three little gold mounts, with a sort
of rounded oval outline, with relief
ornament; in the centre is an oval
opening which probably framed a
cameo or intaglio, held in place by
the little triangular gold teeth which
survive in different numbers
Girona

13.23 MOUNT, Gold
16mm h; .661g
Very small frame from the inside on
a mount, with little triangular gold
teeth
Girona

13.24 MOUNT, Gold with Rubies
33mm high; 2.54g

The remains of a splendid, but badly crushed, gold mount, consisting of an oval frame, on which survives a single triangular gold tooth to hold in place the cameo which was presumably contained there. One raised setting for a gem, still containing a ruby, survives on the outside of the frame

Girona

13.25 NECKLACE OR COLLAR, Gold with Lapis Lazuli and Pearl
41mm l; 10.87g (each)

Eleven of a presumed set of twelve mounts for portrait-cameos of Roman Emperors; six of the blue lapis lazuli portraits survive, the other five are in varying states of preservation. The best preserved, almost in its original condition, still bears at the sides its original complement of four pearls, held on a fine gold wire. At the top of each frame is a little grotesque mask; the shoulders supporting this have a little setting filled with green enamel. The actual cameos are backed by little oval plates of gold, held in place by little triangular teeth. The rings on the backs by which the cameos were connected to one another show that they were worn as a necklace or collar, one on top of the other, six on each side: the ring at the top lies along the long axis, while the ring at the bottom is at right angles to it. A certain controversy exists as to the identity of the Emperors represented: Robert Stenuit considers them to be Byzantine, including Michael I Rhangabe, Stauratius and Constantine II (see colour plate)

Girona

13.26 TOOTH- AND EAR-PICK, Gold
47mm l; 8.99g
Combined tooth- and ear-pick in the
form of a dolphin: the long snout
forms the tooth-pick, the flattened
tail the ear-pick. The dolphin's
nicely modelled eye presumably
watches the entire procedure with
distaste
Girona

13.27 FILIGREE, Gold
20mm d; 1.34g
A circle in filigree consisting of 12
segments, filled with delicate spirals,
all joined together and to a central
circle. Folded in two when found
and subsequently straightened
Girona

13.28 FILIGREE, Gold
11mm l; .172g
A single filigree segment of an
ornament similar to the above
Girona

General Index

All items listed in the catalogue sections of the book are indexed in the separate Catalogue Index.

Catalogue Index